STUDIES IN CHRISTIAN WORSHIP 9

Christmas and Epiphany

Christmas and Epiphany

By JOHN GUNSTONE

THE FAITH PRESS
7 Tufton Street, London, S.W.1

FIRST PUBLISHED IN 1967
© *John Gunstone, 1967*

PRINTED IN GREAT BRITAIN
in 10 point Times Roman
BY THE FAITH PRESS LTD.
LEIGHTON BUZZARD

SBN 7164 0015 4

To Reg and Helen
who took me to Bethlehem

Contents

Thy Nativity, O Christ our God, hath revealed to the world the Light of Wisdom: for in it those who worshipped the stars were taught by a star to adore thee, the Sun of Righteousness, and to know thee, the Dayspring from on high. Glory be to thee, O Lord.

Troparion for the feast of the Nativity of Christ (Orthodox)

When the sun shall have risen from heaven, ye shall see the Kings of kings proceeding from the Father, as a bridegroom out of his bride chamber.

Antiphon to the Magnificat at the first vespers of the feast of the Nativity of our Lord
(Roman)

From early times Christians have speculated about the day of the year on which Jesus Christ was born. A few have wondered if 'the sixth month' in which, Luke tells us, Mary miraculously conceived the Son of God could have been the sixth month of the Jewish year, *Elul* (August–September), fixing the Nativity in May–June. But most commentators have taken the phrase to refer to the sixth month of Elizabeth's pregnancy and reverted to other speculations, based on a mixture of scriptural guesswork and allegorical arithmetic. Clement, Bishop of Alexandria (*d. c.* 215), wrote that some believed May 20th to have been the day, but that his own calculations led him to favour November 18th. Hippolytus (*d. c.* 236) thought that Christ must have been born on the day that God made the sun—the fourth day of the week, a Wednesday—and the *De Pascha Computus,* written in North Africa about 243 and following the same line of thought, argued that, as the first day of creation must have coincided with the vernal equinox, March 25th, our Lord's birthday must be March 28th.

But in the fourth century the Church began to observe December 25th as the feast of the Nativity, and how this came about is the subject of this little book.

We shall trace the emergence of Christmas and Epiphany from their Christian and pagan environment and see how certain biblical themes came to be associated with them. We shall analyse the formularies for the feasts in the Roman missal in the light of this development and assess how they have affected the way in which we keep Christmas in the Church of England. We shall also sketch the traditions behind the season of Advent. Finally, we shall consider a recent attempt to reshape the Christmas cycle for the Church of today.

Practically everything I have written is based on the work of others and my debt to them is indicated very inadequately in the footnotes. But it would have been much more difficult for me to have consulted their books if it had not been for the staff of the Central Library in Romford, who borrowed copies of books and journals for me from all parts of the British Isles. Through their help, I was able to do most of the reading for this essay at home, in odd hours among the everyday activities of a parish priest.

Ascension Day, 1967

Acknowledgments: to Longmans, Green and Co. Ltd. for permission to quote from T. C. Lawler's *St. Augustine's Sermons for Christmas and Epiphany,* to Burns Oates Ltd. for permission to quote from H. Rahner's *Greek Myths and Christian Mystery,* and to the Joint Liturgical Group and the Oxford University Press for permission to quote from *The Calendar and Lectionary.*

I. *The Invincible Sun*

As he contemplated the religious scene of the pagan Roman empire, the Christian who lived in the first decades of the fourth century could have had little doubt about the superiority of his own faith.

Around him he would have seen a vast panorama of ancient cults in varying stages of development or decay.

In the foreground were the state gods, a pantheon which had long been identified with the Greek Olympians. From the time of the republic they had played an important part in binding together the mixed peoples under the rule of the Romans, who found it politically expedient to recognize in local deities manifestations of their own gods. The sentiment inspired by the old gods was cultic rather than religious, but loyalty to them was strong. There was a common feeling that the prosperity of the state depended on the observance of the traditional rituals and the upkeep of the holy places, and well into the Christian era there lingered among the aristocratic classes little clubs who cherished pagan legends and rites as the core and origin of imperial greatness.

Predominant in public life was emperor worship. The victorious Augustus would never have thought of claiming divine status if the eastern provinces, accustomed as they were to worshipping their previous rulers, had not taken the initiative in elevating him to a throne among the immortals, city vying with city for the privilege of erecting a temple to him. He accepted the honour for the obvious advantages it offered, and his successors followed his example. But in the western provinces they were more sceptical. In Rome the few grains of incense scattered on the brazier in the magistrate's office meant no more than the salute which the sailor gives the quarterdeck in the Royal Navy. The attitude of the more sophisticated is reflected in the grim jest of Vespasian who, when he knew that he was dying, whispered, 'I am beginning to turn into a god.'

But the state gods and the shades of the *augusti* did nothing

11

to satisfy that deep and genuine spiritual longing which stirred the peoples of the Mediterranean countries in the second and third centuries A.D. and perhaps earlier. Previously men's hopes had hinged on the cult of the horoscope, the conviction that one's destiny was written in the stars. Now they were in revolt against the tyranny of astrology and seeking a more personal religion, which would bring a release from the pains and evils of the present world and a promise of peace and joy in a life of union with the supreme Deity. They wanted salvation.

It was probably this same longing which had brought our Christian through the long years of the catechumenate to his initiation into the Church—unless he had been born of a Christian family. Others found solace in the mystery religions. Spreading from the east with their wise men and their good tidings of saviours, they could sometimes provide the individual with intense emotional and spiritual experiences. Purifications, lustrations and sacramental banquets were believed to purge humanity of its unworthiness and to release the soul from the imprisonment of the body. Then the Deity could enter in and dwell with his worshippers, filling them with a new sense of holiness and a hope of everlasting life.

Except in the case of the Christian and the Jew, adherence to one mystery religion did not mean infidelity to another. The attitude of the educated was that all religions were divinely inspired and that in their different forms they were suitable for different people. Earnest seekers after truth were initiated into a variety of cults. Apuleius, a traveller in Greece during the second century A.D., seems to have collected them with a fervour not unlike that of a modern philatelist:

'In Greece I took part in very many initiations. I keep carefully certain symbols and memorials of them handed to me by the priests. . . . I learnt worship upon worship, rites beyond number, a great variety of ceremonies, in my zeal for truth and in my dutifulness to the gods.' [1]

Yet the most striking feature in the panorama surveyed by our Christian was the growing synthesis among the state religions and mystery cults, a synthesis which focused on the sun as the highest embodiment of all that man desired. It was as if the blazing orb of the heavens, the most ancient of the

[1] Apuleius, *Apol.,* 55, quoted in Michael Grant, *The World of Rome* (1960).

gods, had become the centre of a massive pagan ecumenical movement. The multitudes of faiths, myths, superstitions, and folklores—from the crudest forms of animism to the most sophisticated philosophical fancies—drew together round *Sol*, the light in the life of every man.

Interpretations of the sun's role varied enormously. He was the night-travelling barque through the Egyptians' world of the dead or the *Helios Pater* of the Greek tragedies; he was venerated as Apollo among the Gauls and as Mithras among soldiers and merchants. Even the emperors in their divine status enjoyed his reflected glory. When Constantius Chlorus, the father of Constantine, entered London in 296, a medal was struck to commemorate the occasion, and on it was engraved a representation of the Caesar arriving at the gate of the city with the words, *Redditor lucis aeternae*, 'Restorer of eternal light' (he had defeated the usurper, Allectus).

Heliolatry could be deeply sincere. Ambrose, Bishop of Milan (*d.* 397), has preserved a hymn to the sun which expresses all the wonder of a genuine devotee:

> *Helios, eye of the world,*
> *Joy of the daytime,*
> *Loveliness of heaven,*
> *Darling of nature,*
> *Jewel of creation!*

And if we are inclined to dismiss this as mere nature worship, then let us compare these lines with Christian antiphons:

> *Helios gives thee release from every pang of the body*
> *Leading thee up to the Father and light eternal of heaven,*

or acknowledge in this stanza a model copied by the Church in her songs to the Lord:

> *Glory of earth and sky,*
> *The sun is the same for all.*
> *Glory of light and darkness,*
> *The sun is the beginning and end.*[2]

[2] Quoted in Hugo Rahner, *Greek Myths and Christian Mystery* (Eng. tr. 1963), pp. 91–2, a book which has supplied much of the material for this chapter. Compare these expressions of devotion with this quotation in a report from Communist China: 'Chairman Mao is the red sun in our hearts, his thoughts shed light all over the world' (*The Christian and Christianity Today*, January 20th, 1967).

13

The solar synthesis of state religions and mystery cults was encouraged by imperial patronage in order to establish a uniform religion throughout the empire. In 274, after his victory at Palmyra, the emperor Aurelian founded a magnificent temple on the *Campus Martius* in Rome in honour of the invincible sun and appointed a college of priests to maintain its offices. He also decreed that December 25th, the *dies natalis Solis invicti,* should be kept as a public holiday. It was a shrewd innovation. Through it the emperor channelized all the instinctive and popular veneration for the sun in its various disguises, and *Sol* was raised to the highest rank in the divine hierarchy. Thus the sun god subordinated to himself all other deities and took under his protection the rulers of Rome and their empire.

The setting up of a new festival was not unknown. Along with the traditional feasts of the gods, such as the *ludi magalenses* in honour of Cybele (April 4th–10th), the *dies natalis* of emperors and other famous personages, and the *feriae publicae,* dates were occasionally set aside for special commemorations. It has been calculated that by the end of the third century there must have been nearly two hundred such holidays in Rome.

But this latest festival was immediately successful. December 25th, the winter solstice in the Julian calendar, had been kept in religious circles previously, but now that it was declared a public holiday all the world flocked to the temples and the bonfires on the day which symbolized rebirth and renewal in life.

The eastern provinces of the empire kept the feast on January 6th—and here we have the origins of the dual Christian celebrations. According to the venerable calendar of Amenemhet I of Thebes (*c.* 1996 B.C.) this was the date of the winter solstice, so it was on this day each year that Alexandria and other provinces in the orient celebrated the rebirth of the sun in the figure of Dionysius or Aion. Decorations, torchlight processions, chanting round the sanctuaries, vigils awaiting the dawn, banquets—all these made up the programme for the day.

Epiphanius, a Palestinian who became Bishop of Salamis in Cyprus in 367, wrote an account of the ceremonies in Alexandria on the night of January 5th–6th:

'The principal of these feasts is that which takes place in

14

the so-called Koreion in Alexandria, this Koreion being a mighty temple in the district sacred to Kore. Throughout the whole night the people keep themselves awake here by singing certain hymns and by means of flute-playing which accompanies the songs they sing to the image of their god. When they have ended these nocturnal celebrations, then at morning cock-crow they descend, carrying torches, into a sort of chapel which is below the ground, and thence they carry up a wooden image of one lying naked upon a bier. This image has upon its forehead a golden cross and two more such seals in the form of crosses, one on each hand, and two further ones, one on each knee, making five such golden seals in all. Then they carry the wooden image seven times round the innermost confines of the temple to the sound of flutes, tambourines and the singing of hymns, and when the procession is over, they return the image to the subterranean place from which it was taken. And if anyone asks them what manner of mysteries these might be, they reply, saying: "Today at this hour Kore, that is the Virgin, has given birth to Aion." ' [3]

January 6th was connected in popular belief with legends of epiphanies by which the gods made themselves known. One concerned the changing of water into wine. Pliny the Elder recorded that on this date Dionysius revealed his presence in different places by transforming water in this way in springs and fountains, and Epiphanius said he knew of this phenomenon in Cilicia and Jerash (the bishop had, apparently, drunk some of this miraculous wine himself!). Originally Dionyius personified the spirit of renewal in nature, but by the Christian era he had come to be identified with *Sol*, and the changing of water into wine was a manifestation of promised richness and joy.

*   *   *   *   *

Exactly how December 25th and January 6th came to be adopted in the Christian calendar we shall never know. The surviving evidence is too fragmentary. But just as a boat, affected by a combination of wind and current, will drift in a certain direction whether or not there is anyone aboard to set the sails or handle the wheel, so the Church was moved by a number of factors which, taken together, resulted in her

[3] Quoted in Rahner, p. 138.

using these dates as celebrations of the fundamental article of her creed.

The first factor was that during the fourth century the Church became part of the Establishment. From the reign of Constantine onwards she began to enjoy imperial favour and the number of converts increased. There were church buildings in the cities, often replacing pagan temples, and the bishops with their teams of clerics were respected and important figures of society. Not only did Christians hold high offices of state, but in some of the provincial centres it was even possible for Christian councillors to perform formal pagan offices (until they were abolished). Once she recovered from the sudden and unexpected persecution of 303–312, the Church grew into the most powerful institution in ordinary life. When Julian, the last of the emperors to devote himself to *Sol*, visited the shrine of Daphne in Antioch to offer sacrifice, he found it dismally neglected by the populace in favour of the martyrium of St. Babylas.

This change in the Church's status gave her a very different attitude towards the things of the world. Formerly, the hope of a Christian had been set on that eternal blessedness of which he could only have a foretaste in this life. He had felt himself to be a stranger and a pilgrim in a foreign land. Now his vision reached earthwards. Constantine's patronage of the Church—a patronage which, in the later years of his reign, included a personal concern for Christian unity, a deep interest in theological conundrums, and a deathbed baptism—affected the Christian's outlook enormously. The follower of Christ saw that the kingdoms of this world might, after all, become outposts of the Kingdom of God.

So the Church adjusted herself to seize the opportunities offered—and inevitably the adjustment involved some accommodation to the world and its forms. Ecclesiastical spheres of pastoral care were drawn round civil boundaries (the parishes), places of worship were modelled on public buildings (the basilicas), and the Christian liturgy appropriated what was useful and acceptable in non-Christian devotion (Ambrose's hymns).[4] The process can be traced in so many

[4] It was on a hymn to the sun that Ambrose modelled his *Splendor paternae gloriae:*

Verusque Sol illabere   'O thou true Sun, on us thy glance
Micans nitore perpeti.   Let fall in royal radiance.'
Trs. Robert Bridges (*English Hymnal*, 52).

areas of the Church's life that it is difficult not to believe that it also lay behind what appears to us as an ecclesiastical take-over bid for December 25th and January 6th.

The second factor was the Church's vocation of proclaiming to the world that Jesus Christ was the only true Light for mankind and that his birth of a virgin mother was the mighty work of God in which all could rejoice. She found herself compelled to insist on this truth particularly on those days when people commemorated or expected the empty signs of *Sol's* coming, for these were the occasions when the human need for the assurance of salvation was widely felt. Like the pagan cults, the Church could also preach a divine *adventus*, but—unlike the cults—she could declare that the One who had come was God himself, manifested in flesh.

In preaching this advent, the Church was able to take up the thought-forms of contemporary mythology and demonstrate how the Gospel fulfilled all that they foreshadowed. The more discerning theologians recognized in the cults a preparation for the Christian truth, a *praeparatio evangelicae*, and this aided the transition from pagan festival to Christian feast.

We can illustrate this kinship of thought and language from the way in which the word *epiphania*, from the stories of divine manifestations in Greek mythology, came to be employed in Israel's scriptures and so also in the New Testament.

In pagan usage *epiphania* denoted the appearances or signs through which the immortals came to the aid of their followers in moments of crisis. The epiphanies of Diana, for example, were famous in the legends of Hellenism. Usually such manifestations were brief affairs and sometimes, like the appearance of Apollo at Delphi, they were commemorated year by year.

Now Judaism, like Hellenism, also had its traditions of God's intervention and commemorated them in annual festivals—the exodus at Passover, the theophany on Sinai at the feast of Weeks, and the dedication of the temple at the feast of Tabernacles. But these manifestations were regarded only as prologues to that greatest and final epiphany on the Day of the Lord, when God would usher in his messianic kingdom and establish his rule for ever. In the scriptures, therefore, *epiphania* and its cognates were employed, not only to

17

denote the manifestations of God in salvation-history, but also to describe the final appearance of God at the end of the age.

The noun, *epiphania,* was not actually used by the Old Testament writers, but its related verb and adjective are common. The verb appears in the Psalms:

'God be merciful unto us, and bless us: and *shew* us the light of his countenance, and be merciful unto us.'

'God is the Lord who hath *shewed* us light.'

The adjective is somewhat misleadingly rendered into English as 'terrible': it means that awesomeness of sinful man in the face of God's holiness and might:

'The day of the Lord is great and very *terrible;*'

'I will send you Elijah the prophet before the great and *terrible* day of the Lord comes.' [5]

But by the time the Book of the Maccabees came to be written, the noun was accepted into scriptural vocabulary in the sense of an intervention by God into present events:

'The *appearances* which came from heaven to those who strove zealously on behalf of Judaism, so that though few in number they seized the whole land.' [6]

In the New Testament these words are associated most frequently with the theme of the Day of the Lord. In the Pauline corpus there are five instances of their use in eschatological passages, as in 2 Thessalonians 2: 8, 'The Lord Jesus will slay him (the lawless one) with the breath of his mouth and destroy him by his *appearing* and his coming.' But in 1 Timothy 3: 16 there is an interesting exception. Here the verb is used to describe the incarnation of the Son of God:

'He *was manifested* in the flesh,

vindicated in the Spirit,

seen by angels,

preached among the nations,

believed on in the world,

taken up in glory.'

Most commentators agree that in these lines the author was quoting an earlier source, perhaps a primitive Christian hymn. Deep in the tradition of the Church's spirituality, therefore, was the idea that Christ's appearance in flesh was the consummation of all epiphanies. Jesus came, said Luke,

[5] Joel 2:11 and Malachi 4:5.

[6] 2 Maccabees 2:21 and in a number of other passages.

perhaps quoting another primitive source, 'to give light (*epiphanai*) to those who sit in darkness,' 'a light for revelation to the Gentiles, and for the glory of thy people, Israel.' December 25th and January 6th in the Christian calendar were from the first festivals of Christ's *appearing*. *Apparitio Domini in carne*, 'the Appearing of the Lord in flesh,' was one of the oldest titles of the feasts.[7]

There has always been a tension in the Church's understanding of the coming of God in flesh and of his coming in judgment on the Last Day. It is not possible to separate all that scripture reveals of the advent of God in history and the eschatological advent of God on which history is converging. In the calendar this tension resolved itself to some extent by transferring the watchfulness for the *parousia* to the season before the festivals in the Christian year, Advent. How the pagan and Christian expectations affected the Church's liturgy during this season is a matter we shall return to in a later chapter.

It is against this background that we must see the great Christological debate within the Church herself which reached its climax between the Council of Nicaea (325) and the Council of Chalcedon (451). Basically it was a debate on how God had manifested himself in flesh. And it is no coincidence that the dates of the two councils almost exactly mark the beginning and the end of that period during which Christmas and Epiphany came to be observed throughout the Church. 'Light of Light, Very God of Very God'—the credal phrases summon like a trumpet the faithful to rejoice in the epiphany of God in flesh and the festivals provided them with the occasion for that rejoicing.

This leads us to the third and final factor. In scripture, and so also in doctrine, the manifestation of God, prefigured in the Old Testament and fulfilled in the New, is frequently portrayed with the use of solar imagery. So the Church was able to challenge the sun-cults in their own language. Indeed, H. Rahner has called the solar expressions of Christian liturgy and devotion 'the homecoming of Helios,' in that all that the sun-devotees longed for was found in the Gospel of

[7] See 'Les Origines de l'Épiphanie et les *Testimonia*' by J. Danielou in *Recherches de Science Religieuse*, 52 (1964), pp. 538–53. The Leonine Sacramentary, the earliest surviving book of the Roman eucharistic liturgy, still has as its proper preface for Christmas, *Hodie via veritatis et vita regni caelestis apparuit.*

the Word made flesh. Malachi prophesied that there would arise 'the sun of righteousness, with healing in his wings,' and the evangelists spoke of Christ as 'the dayspring from on high'—or, literally, as 'the sun-rising from on high'—and as 'the true light that enlightens every man coming into the world.' The author of the Apocalypse had a vision of God 'like the sun shining in full strength.' The Church had but to follow the advice contained in the Book of Wisdom:

'For all men who were ignorant of God . . . supposed that . . . the luminaries of heaven were gods that rule the world. If through delight in the beauty of these things men assumed them to be gods, let them know how much better than these is their Lord, for the author of beauty created them.' [8]

How far Christianity had seized hold of the imagery of the sun-god and appropriated it for her own use can be seen vividly today in the necropolis excavated under St. Peter's in Rome during the search for the apostle's grave. Not far from the traditional site of the tomb there is a small Christian burial chamber of the third century, hemmed in between two pagan mausoleums. The walls of the interior are decorated with biblical themes—fishermen, the Good Shepherd, and Jonah—but in the ceiling there is a splendid mosaic of Helios in his chariot of the sun, drawn by white steeds. His right hand (now lost) must have been raised as a signal for the journey to start. He stands erect, his mantle fluttering in the breeze and his left hand holding the world orb. But it is the nimbus of light rays round his head that reveals his true identity. The lower rays are fashioned into a T cross, a design unknown in earlier pagan examples of this type. The Helios is Christ.[9] No wonder Christian apologists had to deny so often that the members of the Church were not sun-worshippers! [10]

[8] Wisdom 13:1–3.

[9] Engelbert Kirschbaum, *The Tombs of St. Peter and St. Paul* (1959), pp. 36ff. The burial chamber is known as 'M' in the official report. A coloured reproduction appears facing p. 144. A striking transparency of this mosaic is included in the series *Sacre Grotte Vaticane*, obtainable in Rome. Another of the many examples of solar symbolism in early Christian art is the *chrismon*, the pagan sunwheel used to represent the first letter of the Greek *Christos* and the cross: ⊕

[10] Tertullian was only one of the many Christian writers who complained that 'they mistake *Sol* for the Christian God because they have heard that in praying we turn towards the rising sun and because on the day of *Sol* (Sunday) we give ourselves over to joy.'

These seem to be the factors behind the Church's adoption of the two great midwinter festivals of the sun. An older generation of liturgiologists favoured other explanations— L. Duchesne, for instance, thought it probable that December 25th was celebrated as the day of Christ's birth because of astrological and symbolic calculations made by Christians in the early centuries.[11] But modern writers have little doubt that the pagan celebrations are behind Christian festivals. In what may be one of the first Christmas Day sermons we hear the Church's meditation on the solar feast and her resolution to keep it in her own way to the glory of God:

'But they also call (this day) the birthday of the invincible sun. Yet who is so invincible as our Lord who threw down death and conquered him? They may call this day the birthday of *Sol*, yet he alone is the Sun of Righteousness of whom the prophet Malachi said, "There shall arise to you who fear his name the Sun of Righteousness and there shall be healing under his wings." '[12]

And in the rather more extravagant imagery of John Chrysostom, the homecoming of Helios is victoriously announced on Christmas Day:

'Consider what it would mean to see the sun descend from the heavens and walk about the earth. If this could not happen, in the case of the shining body that we can see, without causing all who saw it to be amazed, then think what it means that the Sun of Righteousness should send forth its rays in our flesh and should shine into our souls.'[13]

[11] *Christian Worship: its Origins and Evolution*, pp. 257ff.
[12] Quoted in Rahner, p. 148.
[13] Ibid., p. 154.

II. *The Christian Feasts*

In the fifty years following the Council of Nicaea, Epiphany began to be observed by the Church in the eastern provinces of the empire and Christmas in the western provinces (with a possible exception in Gaul which we will notice in a moment). Then, during the last decade or so of the fourth century and the first decades of the fifth, the Christmas observance spread to the east and the Epiphany observance to the west.

Some Christian communities, having grown accustomed to one festival, resisted the infiltration of the other. In the west the Donatists were criticized by Augustine, Bishop of Hippo (*d*. 430), for not keeping Epiphany, while in the east the Armenians refused to accept Christmas. But by the end of the fifth century both feasts were observed in the major Churches of east and west.

The conservatives can be excused for not welcoming the changes involved. From the second century at least, the Church's calendar had been a very simple affair. Besides the weekly Sundays and the fasts on Wednesdays and Fridays, the only annual observance was the Paschal vigil followed by its fifty days' rejoicing, the primitive season of Pentecost. There was nothing more.

The whole character of the calendar was different from what we know today. Easter Day was not so much a commemoration of Christ's resurrection as the liturgical introduction to a festive season of seven weeks when the members of the Church celebrated their salvation through the total redeeming work of God in Christ. During Pentecost they suspended all fasting and stood for prayer in joy at their baptismal status as God's children by adoption. The great Fifty Days were a foretaste of eternity: Tertullian's 'most joyful season' when the Church realized her union with her Head.

After Nicaea this Pasch-Pentecost was gradually fragmented as the various events in Christian salvation-history were singled out for separate celebrations. The calendar now became more like a series of anniversaries, with special days allocated for the commemoration of the last supper, the passion and death of Christ, the resurrection, the ascension, and the sending of the Holy Spirit. It was as if the whole work of redemption was refracted, like a shaft of light through a prism, so that its separate constituents could be distinguished for different celebrations—although it would be more accurate to describe each day as a celebration of all God had done for man *viewed from the perspective of one particular salvation-event*. This is what has given the feasts of the liturgical year their post-paschal joy. The Church would have nothing to celebrate if she did not know that each event was triumphantly crowned by the resurrection and reign of Christ the King.

Christmas and Epiphany emerged as part of this process of change and elaboration in the Christian calendar.

A convenient way of describing their emergence would be for us to make an imaginary tour of the local Churches round the Mediterranean and to collect the earliest references to the feasts that we can find. Then in the following two chapters we will analyse more closely the *content* of the festivals—that is to say, what was celebrated by the Church on December 25th and January 6th as revealed in the patristic and liturgical texts associated with the two dates.

We will begin our imaginary tour in Rome. Like other Christian communities, the Church in Rome, besides keeping the great festive season of Pasch-Pentecost, also cherished the anniversaries of her own heroes of the faith—the martyrs. The cult had begun in the east. *The Martyrdom of Polycarp*, which must have been written shortly after the bishop's death in 155 or 156, relates how the Smyrnean congregation celebrated his martyrdom each year as a *dies natalis* in the place where they treasured his relics.

Dies natalis—the term was borrowed from pagan sources—meant 'anniversary' in a general sense rather than 'birthday.' The birthdays of famous men were commemorated in Roman calendars, but the term could be applied to other dates as well, and in the Church it came to be used for the anniversary of the martyr's death. In the middle of the third century Cyprian, Bishop of Carthage (*d*. 258), instructed his clergy to keep a register of the members of their congregations who suffered martyrdom or who died in prison, noting the dates. When local Churches revised their lists, they incorporated

23

into them the names and dates of martyrs from neighbouring communities. Cyprian himself was martyred in Carthage but commemorated in Rome less than a century later. It was in this way that the *Sanctorale,* the calendar of the saints, originated.

The first known reference to Christmas Day occurs in the earliest list of martyrs of the Roman Church. This list forms part of what is usually called the Philocalian Calendar, an almanac compiled (or maybe just illuminated) by Furius Dionysius Philocalus, a Greek artist who lived in Rome and who was employed by Pope Damasus (*d.* 384) to engrave inscriptions on martyrs' tombs. The manuscript of this almanac was unfortunately lost in the seventeenth century, but copies are extant reproducing the layout and the illustrations of the original.

The almanac was a comprehensive affair, with lists of the consuls, prefects, bishops and martyrs of Rome, together with a calendar of holidays, a table for finding the date of Easter, a chronicle of secular history, and an account of the fourteen regions of the city. From internal evidence it seems to date from about 354. It was dedicated *Floreas in Deo, Valentine,* 'Valentinus, may you prosper in God,' so it must have been commissioned as a sumptuous New Year's gift to a Roman citizen who, although he was a Christian, needed civil and other information available for reference.

At the top of the list of martyrs, which was probably taken by the compiler from a source twenty years older than the almanac itself, are these words:

idem depositio martyrum:
VIII Kal. Ianu. Natus Christus in Bethleem Iudaea.

'Burial of martyrs:
On the eighth day of the Calends of January, Christ born in Bethlehem of Judaea.'

The Julian calendar retained the ancient custom of numbering the days according to the lunar month. As the Calends of January were the days in December following the new moon, the eighth day was December 25th.

In the almanac's list of consuls it is stated:

Caesare et Paulo. Sat. XIII. Hoc cons. dominus Jesus
Christus natus est VIII Kal. Ian. d. Ven. luna XV.

'Caesar and Paul (being consuls), (January 1st fell on) the day of Saturn (Saturday), the 13th of the moon. In this consulate Jesus Christ our Lord was born on the eighth day of the Calends of January, a day of Venus (Friday), the 15th of the moon.' [1]

By the 330s, then, December 25th was kept in Rome as the anniversary of Christ's birth—a date which, according to the almanac, was believed to correspond with the actual day on which he had been born. But from the factors we have considered in the last chapter, it was almost certainly fixed on this date because of the *natalis solis invicti*.

The years from which the extract originated—the 330s—also saw the end of Constantine's reign, and inevitably this raises the question, Was the emperor responsible in any way for promoting the Christian observance of December 25th? We know that he made it possible for the Church to worship on the weekly Lord's Day, for he promulgated a decree concerning 'the venerable day of the sun.' And we know that with his mother, Helena, he was interested in the circumstances of the Saviour's birth, for he arranged for a basilica to be constructed over the grotto of the Nativity at Bethlehem. Furthermore, the fact that December 25th was kept as a religious festival by almost every subject in the western empire may well have prompted him to encourage its observance by the Church. Whatever his own beliefs Constantine, like any other ruler, could not overlook the obvious advantages of uniting his people in a common and popular festal day, meaningful to Christian and non-Christian alike.

Mme. Denis-Boulet has suggested that the building of St. Peter's in Rome, another of Constantine's benefactions, may have been the occasion for inaugurating the celebration of Christmas. She has pointed out that on the Vatican hill in pagan times there was a temple to which the inhabitants of Rome flocked on the day of the winter solstice and that this temple was not far from the traditional grave of the apostle. (Its proximity, she adds, may well have inspired the artist who executed the mosaic of the Christ-Helios in the mausoleum described in the previous chapter.) The building of the

---

[1] These extracts are copied in most books on the liturgical year. I have used the version and translation in N. M. Denis-Boulet, *The Christian Calendar* (1960).

basilica over the apostle's grave, which the emperor ordered to begin in the 320s, may therefore have served a double purpose: to honour the apostle's relics, and to divert the homage that people were accustomed to give to the temple on the hill to the new Christian sanctuary.[2] Even in Leo's time, a century later, the pope had to rebuke the congregation coming to the basilica on Christmas Day for persisting in pagan habits: some of them still paused at the top of the steps and turned to bow to the rising sun before entering the atrium!

But all this is very speculative. The most we can suggest is that if Constantine found among his Christian advisers a movement to observe December 25th as a festival, it is quite likely he would have given the movement his support.

So Christians in Rome began to celebrate the *natalis Christi* in the second quarter of the fourth century. But when did they begin to keep Epiphany? The earliest definite date is the pontificate of Leo the Great (440–461), who preached at mass on this festival in a manner which suggests that the celebration was a comparatively recent innovation. C. Coebergh, however, has tried to pinpoint evidence to show that Epiphany was introduced into the Roman Church at least twenty years earlier and his discussion is worth following.[3]

His clue is in the correspondence between the emperor Honorius in Ravenna and Symmachus, the prefect of Rome, on the problem caused by the election of rival popes after the death of Zosimus in 418. What had happened was that one group of Roman churchmen had collected at the Lateran after the funeral of Pope Zosimus on December 27th and elected the archdeacon, Eulalius, as their bishop, while on the next day the cardinal presbyters had met in another church to choose their fellow-priest Boniface. Fearing a repetition of the riot that had occurred fifty years' previously during the disputed election of Damasus, the prefect wrote to the emperor in Ravenna seeking advice and received a reply dated January 3rd. In his further report to Honorius on January 8th, Symmachus mentioned the fact that both Eula-

[2] N. M. Denis-Boulet, *Recherches de Science Religieuse,* 34 (1947), pp. 385–406.

[3] Fr. Coebergh's article is in *Revue Bénédictine* 75 (1965). Honorius' letters are printed in P. R. Coleman-Norton, *Roman State and Christian Church,* 2 (1966), pp. 586ff.

lius and Boniface with their supporters had kept the 'solemnity of the holy day,' one at St. Peter's and the other at St. Paul's-without-the-Walls.[4]

But, asks Fr. Coebergh, what *sollemnitas* was this? Honorius' reply of January 3rd would have taken at least two days to travel by courier along the *cursus publicus* from Ravenna to Rome (the route went through Rimini, down the Adriatic coast and across the mountains by the Flaminia Via) so it could not have been in Symmachus' hands before the 5th, a Sunday. Now although the prefect was not a Christian, it is unlikely that he would have referred to the weekly Lord's Day as a *sollemnitas*. Sunday was well established by then and would hardly have been referred to in that way. Therefore, argues Fr. Coebergh, the phrase in Symmachus' report of the 8th must refer to some festival kept on the 6th or the 7th—and the most probable one was Epiphany on the 6th.

Fr. Coebergh goes on to ask who could have introduced this festival to Rome. Although Zosimus was of Greek origin and so would have known the oriental feast, his pontificate from 417 to 418 was too short for him to have made any important liturgical innovations—and the fact that both Eulalius and Boniface felt obliged to assert their status by keeping the feast in the city's major basilicas indicates that it must have been kept for some years previously. Fr. Coebergh's candidate for the honour of introducing Epiphany to Rome is Zosimus' predecessor, Innocent I (410–417). This pope is known to have been interested in liturgical affairs.

Across the Mediterranean in North Africa we hear of an early Christmas sermon given by Optatus, Bishop of Milevis, about the year 360. He spoke of the adoration of the magi and the massacre of the innocents as well as the birth of Christ—a not unusual combination of subjects on such an occasion for, as we shall see, the primitive Christmas in the west was a celebration of Christ's appearance and of the various episodes connected with it as well as a celebration of his birth. Fifty years later Augustine preached both at Christmas and Epiphany. In 412 he criticized the Donatists for not keeping Epiphany: 'They neither love unity, nor are they in communion with the eastern Church where that star appeared'

4 *Eo tempore . . . quo sancti diei erat celebranda sollemnitas.*

27

—indicating that he knew of the oriental origins of the feast.[5] Communications between ports like Carthage and Ostia were excellent—North Africa was the granary of ancient Rome—and we would expect the Christian communities in the two areas to follow each others' customs fairly closely.

Moving to northern Italy we find Philaster, Bishop of Brescia (*d. c.* 397), listing four feasts—Christmas, Epiphany, Easter and Pentecost, with an additional reference to Ascension Day in another version of the text, in his book on heresies. He also mentioned four fasts in preparation for these celebrations. The book was written between 385 and 391. Maximus, Bishop of Turin (*d. c.* 470), opened his address on Christmas Day with these words:

'It is not surprising that people should call the Lord's birthday "the day of the new sun (*sol novus*)." Let us feel free to copy them, for in the Saviour's rising not only is mankind's salvation renewed but also the sun's brightness. . . . If the sun grew dark when Christ suffered, it must then shine more brightly when he was born.' [6]

The interpretation of the feast had turned a full circle. The sun was renewed on December 25th *because* it was the birthday of Christ! Hence Maximus could view the pagan customs with equanimity!

Crossing the Alps into Gaul, the first reference to our feasts is not to Christmas but to Epiphany. In his *Res Gestae,* explaining how Julian maintained the outward practice of Christian observances at his accession in 361 for political motives, Ammianus Marcellinus noted that the emperor went to church 'on the day of the festival in January which Christians call Epiphany.' [7] Julian was in Vienne at the time. The chronicler, who was a pagan, did not mention Christmas, and although this does not mean that December 25th was not kept in Gaul as well as January 6th, it is quite likely that the

[5] *Sermons for Christmas and Epiphany,* ed. T. C. Lawler (Ancient Christian Writers, 15, 1952), p. 170. Does this imply that the Donatists only kept Christmas because this feast was observed by the Church before they went into schism between 305 and 312, whereas Epiphany was introduced later? Some scholars have argued this way and claimed that Christmas was kept in Rome and north Africa at the end of the third century, soon after Aurelian instituted the festival of the sun. But such an early dating is, as H. Rahner, one of its exponents, admits, 'a little bold.'

[6] *Patrologia Latina,* ed. J. P. Migne (1844ff.), 57, 537.

[7] Bk. xxi, ch. ii.

Church in that province began observing Epiphany before it observed Christmas. It is one of the well known features of liturgical history that the early Gallican Church followed more closely the customs of the eastern Church than those of its nearer neighbours. The old oriental title for January 6th, 'the Theophany,' remained attached to the feast day in Gaul long after it was used in the east to denote Christmas day as well.

John Cassian wrote in his *Conferences:* 'The clergy of Egypt observe the feast of the Epiphany as the time of our Lord's birth as well as the time of his baptism and, unlike the western Church with its two separate festivals, keep both commemorations on the same day. They keep a custom of immemorial antiquity, that after Epiphany the Bishop of Alexandria sends a letter to every church and monastery in Egypt declaring the date for the beginning of Lent and Easter Day.' [8]

On the face of it, this quotation really belongs to our discussion on eastern observances. The *Conferences* purport to describe life in the Egyptian monasteries which Cassian visited before settling at Marseilles at the beginning of the fifth century. But since this book was written at least twenty years after his arrival in the west, it is quite possible that Cassian's description also applies to the Gallican Church with which he had become familiar.

Further west, the Synod of Saragosa (380) laid down that no one should absent himself from church between December 17th and January 6th. The provision was probably designed to counteract the lure of the *saturnalia,* which began in the middle of December, but it indicates that Epiphany was a festival with a preparatory period of three weeks.

To sum up the evidence we have collected in our imaginary tour of the western half of the empire, then, Rome and North Africa seem to have begun keeping Christmas during the first half of the fourth century and over the turn of the century began observing Epiphany as well. In Gaul and Spain, however, Epiphany seems to have been kept first, though the Church in these countries accepted Christmas by the fifth

[8] *Western Ascetism,* ed. O. Chadwick (*Library of Christian Classics,* 12, 1953), pp. 233–4. The Roman *Pontificale* contains a form of announcing the dates of the feasts for use at Epiphany.

century. In northern Italy both feasts were observed by the end of the fourth century.

* * * * *

The eastern half of our tour begins at Alexandria, for here as early as the beginning of the third century Bishop Clement, discussing the date of Christ's birth, wrote: 'The followers of Basilides keep as a festival the day of Jesus' baptism and spend the whole of the preceding night in readings. According to them, this took place in the fifteenth year of Tiberius Caesar on the fifteenth day of the month *Tubi*—others say on the eleventh day.' [9] These dates are January 10th and 6th respectively. Was this an early observance of Epiphany? Clement's reference to a night spent in readings sounds very much like the vigil which preceded the festival in the east. But would Epiphany have been kept among the heretics before it was observed by the orthodox Christians? Basilides was the leader of a Gnostic sect which flourished in Alexandria between 120 and 140. It taught that the Son of the Father had united himself to the human nature of Jesus at his baptism in the river Jordan—a tenet common among those who held adoptionist views of the incarnation. Nothing more is known of this sect. As for its festival, all we can say is that if this was a primitive Epiphany observance, then it was a long time before it was copied elsewhere. On the whole it seems more accurate to interpret this reference as an illustration of the influence of paganism on a heretical sect rather than a very early observance of the Christian festival.

The first evidence for the feast of Epiphany in Egypt—if the dating is right—is a papyrus containing a liturgical formulary of readings and responses. O. Cullmann, who quotes from it in his essay on the origins of Christmas, ascribes it to the fourth century. When the scriptures had been read telling of Christ's birth at Bethlehem, the flight into Egypt and the return to Nazareth, the choir sang in Greek:

> 'Born at Bethlehem,
> Brought up at Nazareth,
> Dwelt in Galilee.'

[9] *Stromata* i, xxi (Ante-Nicene Christian Library, 4 [1867], p. 445).

Then, after the story of the adoration of the magi from Matthew, they responded:

> 'We have seen a sign from heaven,
> The shining star.'

Finally there was a lesson from St. Luke 2, and the choir sang:

> 'Shepherds in the field tending their flocks were amazed,
> They fell on their knees, and sang:
>> "Glory to the Father.
>> Alleluia.
>> Glory to the Son, and to the Holy Ghost.
>> Alleluia. Alleluia. Alleluia." ' [10]

Together with the reference in Cassian's *Conferences* of Epiphany as a commemoration of Christ's birth and baptism, this seems to indicate that the feast began to be observed in Egypt at about the same time that Christmas began to be kept in Rome. The baptism in the Jordan was, as we shall see, an important Epiphany theme in the east.

Christmas was not kept by the Church of Alexandria until the following century. Its adoption may have been symptomatic of the reaction against Nestorianism, a heresy attributed to the man who became Bishop of Constantinople in 428, and who criticized the title of 'God-bearer,' *Theotokos*, for the Virgin Mary. The case against Nestorius was taken up by Cyril, Bishop of Alexandria (*d.* 444), who was moved as much by the rivalry which existed between his see and that of Constantinople as by any love of orthodox teaching. Focusing as it did on the birth at Bethlehem, the western festival was a valuable teaching aid with which to stress the doctrine of the Word made flesh.

The popularization of the observance in Alexandria may well have been due to Cyril's personal initiative. How successful he was is hinted at in the transcript made by a scribe when Paul, Bishop of Emesa, preached at Alexandria one Christmas in the presence of Cyril. He declared:

'This day a wondrous child is born; and the delivery of the Virgin that "knew not man" has come to pass. O wonderful event! a virgin brings forth, and remains a virgin.'

[10] O. Cullmann, *The Early Church* (Eng. tr. 1956), p. 26.

And the scribe noted that at that point the congregation shouted out:

'This is our faith! This is the gift of God!'[11]

Do we detect an echo of that same excitement shown by their forefathers at the birth of Aion?

We move on from Alexandria to Jerusalem. During the fourth century the Holy City was slowly rising to a position of unique importance in Christendom. Aelia Capitolina, which Hadrian had founded on the ruins left after the Barcochba revolt, had contained only a tiny community of Gentile Christians, but by the time of the Council of Nicaea things had begun to change. One of the council's canons had laid down that on grounds of custom and ancient tradition, the Bishop of Jerusalem should have a special place of honour in the Church, and in the following century at the Council of Chalcedon (451) the Jerusalem bishopric was granted patriarchal rank.

It was the patronage of Constantine and his mother that initiated this change in Jerusalem's status. In his policy of establishing the Christian faith as the chief religion of the empire, the emperor aimed at promoting the Holy City as a centre of pilgrimage and a focus of unity, and the new basilicas, built in Jerusalem and at Bethlehem at public expense as part of his scheme, provided the Church there with a magnificent opportunity for developing and elaborating liturgical customs in close association with the actual places named in the Gospel. From the glorious mosaic floor of the church in Bethlehem, for example, worshippers were able to look down into the cave where Christ was believed to have been born. The idea of celebrating the Nativity at Bethlehem on a suitable occasion was irresistible. Credit for these liturgical experiments is given by most scholars to Cyril, who was Bishop of Jerusalem from about 349 until his death in 386.

Pilgrims began arriving in greater numbers. Egeria, a nun from Spain who visited the Holy Land about 385, found that the Nativity of Christ was celebrated in Bethlehem with a nocturnal vigil and a eucharist on January 5th–6th. Unfortunately, the leaves in her diary which describe the service have been lost, and we can only pick up her narrative at the

[11] M. F. Toal, *The Sunday Sermons of the Great Fathers,* 1 (1955), p. 122.

point where she was in the procession accompanying the bishop back to Jerusalem on the morning of the Epiphany. She tells us, however, that 'in Bethlehem through the entire eight days the feast is celebrated in festal array and joyfulness by the priests and all the clerics there and the monks who are stationed in that place.' [12]

When Jerome settled in Bethlehem in 386 he brought with him the Roman custom of celebrating the Nativity of Christ on December 25th and he had to reprove his monks for assuming that, because they happened to live in the place where Christ was born, their traditional date for the birth was more authentic. Science was on Jerome's side, for he was able to point to the fact that December 25th was the true winter solstice, not January 6th:

'Even creation justifies our preaching and the cosmos witnesses to the truth of our words. Up until now the days have continued to wane, but from this day onwards the darkness grows less. The light increases, the nights diminish. The day grows greater, and error shrinks; up rises truth. For today there is born unto us the Sun of Righteousness.' [13]

But in spite of the presence of westerners like Jerome, Jerusalem followed Alexandria in not immediately copying the feast of December 25th. The Armenian Lectionary, which reflects the use of the Church in Jerusalem a hundred years after Egeria's pilgrimage, mentions casually that 'in other towns is kept the Nativity of Christ' but that in the Holy City December 25th is a commemoration of 'James and David.' [14] It was not until the second half of the sixth century that Christmas Day was observed there.

The Churches of Cappadocia seem to have accepted the western festival along with Epiphany more readily than Alexandria or Jerusalem. Basil, Bishop of Caesarea, preached a Christmas sermon between 370 and 378, and when Gregory, Bishop of Nyssa, came to Caesarea to deliver the oration at Basil's funeral on January 1st, 381, he mentioned the feast of the Nativity as if it was an observance with which everyone was familiar. In 379 or 380 Gregory, Bishop of Nazianzus,

[12] From the extracts of Egeria's diary printed in an appendix to L. Duchesne's *Christian Worship: its Origins and Evolution* (Eng. tr. 1904), p. 552.
[13] Quoted in Rahner, pp. 148–9.
[14] F. C. Conybeare, *Rituale Armenorum* (1905).

33

C

also delivered a Christmas homily using the title 'Theophany' —a term usually associated with Epiphany:

'Christ is born . . . the festival is the "Theophany" or "Birthday," for it is called both—two titles being given to the same thing. For God was manifested to man by birth. . . . The name Theophany is given to it in reference to the manifestation, and that of Birthday in respect of his birth. This is our present festival; it is this which we are celebrating today —the coming of God to man.' [15]

Twelve days later he explained to the congregation in Constantinople the significance of the Epiphany:

'The holy day of lights, to which we have come and which we are celebrating today, has for its origin the baptism of my Christ, the true Light that lightens every man coming into the world, and effects my purification. . . . It is a season of new birth: let us be born again! We duly celebrated at his birth —I, the one who presided at the feast, and you, and all that is in the world and above the world. With the star we ran, with the magi we worshipped, with the shepherds we were enlightened, with the angels we glorified him, with Simeon we took him up in his arms, and with the chaste and aged Anna we made our responsive confession. . . . Now we come to another of Christ's acts and another mystery . . . the Spirit bears witness to his Godhead, for he descends upon One that is like him, as does the Voice from heaven. . . . Let us venerate today the baptism of Christ! ' [16]

The evidence of John Chrysostom's sermons is confusing. On Whitsunday 386 he referred to three festivals in the liturgical year, Pentecost, Pasch and Epiphany, in that order —the latter being 'the first of the Christian festivals.' But in another homily, preached at a commemoration of the martyr Philogonium on December 20th, he described Christmas as the feast on which all the others depended. Then, again, in a sermon delivered on Christmas Day in the same year he revealed that it was a comparatively recent innovation:

'It is not yet the tenth year since this day has become

[15] *Nicene and Post-Nicene Fathers*, 7 (1894), p. 345.
[16] In his *Les Origines de la Noël et de l'Épiphany* (1932) B. Botte suggested that Gregory meant he had introduced the feast to Constantinople and was therefore its 'leader'; but A. A. McArthur is surely right when he points out that *exarchos* can also mean 'one who presides': *The Evolution of the Christian Year* (1953), p. 47.

clearly known to us. . . . And so this day, too, which has been known from of old to the inhabitants of the west, and has now been brought to us, not many years ago, has developed so quickly and has manifestly proved so fruitful.' [17]

The Apostolic Constitutions, which originated in Syria at the end of the fourth century, make provisions for both Christmas and Epiphany in a form of calendar that reckons April as the first month of the year:

'Brethren, observe the festival days; and first of all the Birthday which you are to celebrate on the twenty-fifth of the ninth month; after which let the Epiphany be to you the most honoured, in which the Lord made to you a display of his own Godhead, and let it take place on the sixth of the tenth month.' [18]

How are we to interpret the writings attributed to Ephraem the Syrian (d. c. 373)? The nineteen hymns for the Nativity of Christ and the fifteen hymns for the feast of the Epiphany are rich in devotional and interpretative comment, but it is doubtful if they can all be attributed directly to him and presented as evidence of observances by the Church in Edessa, where he lived from about 363. We will, however, quote from one hymn which draws out the solar background of the feasts and comments allegorically on the twelve days separating the two dates:

'The sun conquers
And the steps by which it approaches its zenith
Show forth a mystery.
Lo! It is twelve days since he began to mount upward
And today is the thirteenth day.
It is the perfect symbol of the Son and his twelve
    apostles.
The darkness of winter is conquered,
To show that Satan is conquered.
The sun conquers, so that all may know
That the only-begotten Son of God triumphs over all.' [19]

The Armenian Church has never observed December 25th. That section of it which is in communion with Rome accepted the feast into its calendar during the sixteenth century, but only after some resistance to papal pressure. Yet even today

[17] Quoted in McArthur, p. 50.
[18] ANCL, 17, p. 130.
[19] Quoted in Rahner, p. 145.

the Latin Armenians still regard Epiphany as the principal feast, and their preparatory five days of abstinence and their octave are centred on January 6th, not Christmas Day.

In time, December 25th may have come to be regarded as the true anniversary of Christ's birth, but eastern Christians were still inclined to excuse the priority of their own festival. Bar Salibi, a Syrian writer, explained it this way:

'The reason why the Fathers changed this feast from 6th January to 25th December was, it is said, as follows: The heathen were accustomed on 25th December to celebrate the feast of the birthday of the sun and to light fires in honour of that day, and even Christians were invited to take part in these festivities. When the doctors of the Church observed that Christians were being induced to participate in these practices, they decided to celebrate this day as the true anniversary of Christ's birth and to keep 6th January for the celebration of the feast of the Epiphany, and this custom continued to be observed to the present day together with the practice of lighting fires.' [20]

[20] Ibid., p. 152.

III. *Christmas Day*

It was no coincidence that the champions of orthodoxy in the Christological debates of the fourth and fifth centuries—the Cappadocian Fathers in the east and Augustine and Leo in the west—were among those chiefly responsible for giving Christmas and Epiphany their special significance in the Church's liturgical year. For what is most vital in theology is always inspired by pastoral need. The doctrines asserted at the councils about Jesus Christ and his relationship with the Persons of the Blessed Trinity were formulated in the everyday task of leading to faith in the incarnate Lord the thousands of ordinary folk who worshipped in the bishops' basilicas. To teach that faith the pastors of the Church urged their congregations to keep the feasts, reading to them and expounding the scriptural passages from which this cornerstone of Christian dogma is hewn. This is why Christmas and Epiphany became major celebrations.

The theology of the Incarnation was discussed by the Fathers in numerous homilies and books, but in this and the following chapter we shall as far as possible confine ourselves to quotations taken from sermons delivered on the actual feast days.

Christmas Day was for the Fathers above all the time when the Church contemplated the appearance of the Lord in flesh at Bethlehem. Consequently it was a day when Christians shared in the joy of the angels and shepherds.

'With the shepherds join in praising God,' said Gregory of Nazianzus (*d*. 389), 'with the angels sing hymns, and with archangels make a chorus.' [1]

The symbolism of the new light, associated with December 25th as the day of the sun's birth, was an expression of this joy. Augustine took up this symbolism and presented it as a sign of God's glory manifested in the divine nativity:

'The day of his birth shows the mystery of his light. The apostle indicates this when he says, "The night is passed, and

[1] NPNF, 7, p. 351.

the day is at hand. Let us cast off the works of darkness, and put on the armour of light. Let us walk honestly, as in the day." Let us recognize that it is day. Let us be day ourselves. When we were living without faith, we were night. And, because this same lack of faith, which covered the whole world like the night, had to be lessened by the growth of faith, so on the birthday of our Lord Jesus Christ the nights began to be shorter, while the days became longer.' [2]

The Bishop of Hippo underlined the moral implications of what was celebrated. Christmas was for him more than an assurance of God's presence in the world; it was also a challenge to man's conduct—as a realization that 'we who were "heretofore darkness" are made "light in the Lord." '

The emergence of Christmas gave the homilists an opportunity of explaining all that is implied in Christ's birth. The heresies which claimed that Jesus was not truly God or that he was not truly man were refuted. In his sermon on the feast John Chrysostom wrestled with the truth of the Incarnation as it was taught in scripture and defined in the creeds:

'This day he who is, is born; and he who is, becomes what he was not. For when he was God, he became man; yet not departing from the Godhead that is his. Nor yet by any loss of divinity became he man, nor through increase became he God from man; but, being the Word, he became flesh—his nature, because of impassibility, remaining unchanged.' [3]

Augustine showed that the birth of Christ was an expression of the Son's procession from the Father within the Trinitarian Godhead:

'It was one and the same who from all time and for ever is the Son of God begotten of the Father, who began to be the Son of man by his birth of the Virgin. And thus, too, was human nature added to the Son's divine nature. Yet the result was not a quarternity of persons, but the Trinity remains.'

'Let us, then, Christians, celebrate this day,' he said another year, 'not as that of his divine birth, but of his human birth, namely, the birth by which he spared us, so that through the

[2] *Sermons*, pp. 101–2.

[3] Toal, p. 110. The authenticity of this homily has been questioned, but most scholars accept it as a work of John Chrysostom. It is possible, however, that the passage I have quoted is an addition to the original by Cyril of Alexandria.

invisible made visible, we may pass from visible things to the invisible. With our Catholic faith we ought to hold fast that the Lord has two births, the one divine, the other human; the one timeless, the other in time. Both, moreover, are extraordinary: the one without a mother, the other without a father.'[4]

In his Christmas sermon before Cyril of Alexandria, Paul of Emesia also stressed the perfect union of the divine and human natures in the womb of the *Theotokos*.

'Mary, the Mother of God, has borne unto us Emmanuel: Emmanuel, who is God made man. For God the Word, who in a mysterious and unspeakable manner was begotten by the Father before all ages, in these days was born of a woman. For having perfectly assumed our nature, and uniting mankind to himself from the moment of his conception, and making our body a temple for himself, he came forth from the Virgin fully God, and the same is fully man. For the meeting of two perfect natures, the divine and the human, has given us one Son, one Christ, one Lord.'[5]

This led to one of the favourite Christmas themes—the amazing mystery that the Creator of the world should submit to his creation by becoming a part of it. The preachers loved to turn this theme through all its infinite variations and there is hardly an early sermon on the feast that does not express it in one form or another.

'The Ancient of days has become an infant!' exclaimed John Chrysostom. 'He who sits upon the high and heavenly throne now lies in a cradle! He who cannot be touched is now fondled by human hands! He who has broken the bonds of sinners is now bound by swaddling clothes!'[6]

Augustine made a great play on the paradoxes. Even though this passage has been translated, we still catch the grandeur of his oratory:

'The Word of God before all time, the Word made flesh at a suitable time. Maker of the sun, he is made under the sun. Disposer of all ages in the bosom of the Father, he consecrates this day in the womb of his mother; in him he remains, from her he goes forth. Creator of heaven and earth, he was born on earth under heaven. Unspeakably wise, he is

[4] *Sermons,* pp. 81 and 102.
[5] Toal, p. 122.
[6] Ibid., p. 112.

wisely speechless; filling the world, he lies in a manger; ruler of the stars, he nurses at his mother's bosom. He is both great in the nature of God, and small in the form of a servant, but so that his greatness is not diminished by his smallness, nor his smallness overwhelmed by his greatness. For he did not desert his divine works when he took to himself human members. Nor did he cease "to reach from end to end mightily, and to order all things sweetly," when, having put on the infirmity of the flesh, he was received into the Virgin's womb, not confined therein.' [7]

The north African theological school maintained that the sinful traits of man were transmitted from Adam to succeeding generations through the sexual union of men and women, and Augustine laid strong emphasis on the virginity of Mary as a necessary precondition of the Son of man's perfection. In his Christmas sermons he exalted the Virgin as the model of chastity. Following him, Leo explained in his homilies on the Nativity that because 'in all mothers conception does not take place without the stain of sin,' Christ was conceived virginally so that he could bring 'to men's bodies the new gift of unsullied purity.' This idea lies behind the doctrine of original sin in the western Church, but its positive contribution to the Christmas celebration was that it led to an exposition of the Incarnation as the renewal and rebirth of the entire human race. 'The Word was united with the flesh,' as Ephraem had said, 'and in return he clothed that flesh with its true splendour, majesty and dignity.' [8]

The Virgin's womb, then, was what the Byzantine liturgy called 'the nuptial chamber of immortality'—the place where the marriage of the divine and human natures was solemnized in the power of the overshadowing Spirit. Psalms 19 and 85 provided Augustine with appropriate phraseology:

'No one was to despise Truth,' he said, 'because it is "sprung out of the earth," when like a bridegroom it came out of its bride chamber, that is, out of the Virgin's womb where the Word of God was united to human creation by a marriage which it is impossible to define.' [9]

[7] *Sermons*, p. 85.

[8] Quoted in J. Lemarié, *La Manifestation du Seigneur: la Liturgie de Noël et de l'Épiphanie* (1957), p. 159. In this and the following chapter, I have taken many quotations from this fascinating book, especially passages from Eastern liturgies.

[9] *Sermons*, p. 115.

40

So at Christmas the Church was led to rejoice in what the antiphon of vespers for the feast of the Circumcision in the Roman rite calls the *admirabile commercium:*

'O wonderful exchange: the Creator of the human race, taking unto himself a living body, deigns to be born of a Virgin: and becoming man from human generation, hath bestowed upon us his divinity.'

It is a liturgical celebration of the theory of recapitulation. This theory, which is familiar to students of Christian doctrine, envisages Christ as the representative of the entire human race. Just as all men were somehow present in Adam, so they are—or can be—present in the second Adam, the man from heaven.

The theory runs through many patristic sources: 'He was incarnate and made man; and then he recapitulated in himself the long line of the human race, procuring for us a comprehensive salvation, that we might recover in Christ Jesus what in Adam we had lost, namely, the state of being in the image and likeness of God' (Irenaeus); 'The Word who proceeds from God the Father was born among us after the flesh so that we also could be born of God through the Spirit' (Cyril); 'God became man that man might become God' (Augustine).[10] And it was expressed devotionally in that Leonine collect which, although not found in the Roman missal, was fortunately rescued by the compilers of the 1928 Prayer Book for use in Christmastide.

'Almighty God, who didst wonderfully create man in thine own image, and didst yet more wonderfully restore him: Grant, we beseech thee, that as thy Son our Lord Jesus Christ was made in the likeness of men, so we may be made partakers of the divine nature.' [11]

Christmas, then, is more than a celebration of Christ's nativity; it is also a celebration of a Christian's own rebirth in Christ, his participation in the divine nature through the

[10] J. N. D. Kelly, *Early Christian Doctrines* (1958), pp. 170ff.

[11] Collect for Christmas II. Though not actually a collect in the Roman missal, the formula is preserved in the prayer said by the celebrant at mass when he pours the wine and the water into the chalice at the offertory: 'O God, who didst wonderfully create, and yet more wonderfully renew the dignity of man's nature: grant that by the mystery of this water and wine we may be made partakers of his divinity, who vouchsafed to share our humanity, Jesus Christ thy Son our Lord.'

baptismal covenant. Gregory of Nazianzus' homily for the feast demonstrates this palpably:

'Today we celebrate the coming of God to us in order that we should come to him—or, rather, in order that we should come back to him—so that, putting off the old man, we should put on the new. As we were dead in the old Adam, so let us live in Christ, being born with him, crucified with him, buried with him, risen with him.' [12]

'Let us celebrate on this day the redemption of the world,' said Basil. 'Let us keep this day as that of humanity's birth. Today the condemnation of Adam is lifted. Henceforth no one can say, "Dust thou art, and unto dust shalt thou return." For you have been united with the heavenly man and you will be received into heaven.' [13]

This accounts for the references to a Christian's baptismal adoption as a son of God which occur frequently in the sermons and liturgical texts at Christmas time. 'To everyone when he is reborn,' preached Leo, 'the water of baptism is like the Virgin's womb; for the same Holy Spirit fills the font who filled the Virgin, that the sin which that sacred conception overthrew may be taken away by this mystical washing.' [14]

The epistle for the feast of the Nativity in the Milanese and Syrian rites is Galatians 4 ('God sent forth his Son, made of a woman, made under the law, to redeem them that were under the law, that we might receive the adoption of sons . . .'). The Roman missal and the Prayer Book set this pericope as the lesson for the Sunday after Christmas, but it is echoed in the collect for Christmas Day in the Prayer Book, which asks God to grant 'that we being regenerate (that is, baptized) and made thy children by adoption and grace, may daily be renewed by thy Holy Spirit.'

Mary's role at Bethlehem mirrors the vocation of the Church in all ages and at all places. By baptism the Church gives birth to new sons of God as at Christmas Mary gave birth to the Son of God. One year on the feast of the Nativity, Augustine drew out the parallel:

'This is he who is "beautiful above the sons of men," Son of holy Mary, Bridegroom of holy Church whom he has made

12 NPNF, 7, pp. 345–6.
13 PG, 31, 1473.
14 NPNF, 12, p. 135.

like his own mother; for he has given her to us to be our mother and keeps her a virgin for himself. It is to her that the apostle says, "I have prepared you for one husband that I may present you as a chaste virgin to Christ." And concerning her he says again that our mother is not a bond-woman, but a freewoman, and "many are the children of the desolate, more than of her that hath a husband." The Church, too, then, like Mary, has perpetual virginity and inviolate fecundity. For what Mary has merited in the flesh, the Church has preserved in the soul. But whereas the one gave birth to only One, the other gives birth to many, who through the One are to be gathered into one.' [15]

From such an outlook as this, we might have expected Christmas to have become a baptismal day, but Rome clung to the older tradition of baptizing only at Easter and Whitsunday. Leo was probably the last of the popes to uphold this discipline. The oriental custom of administering the sacrament at Epiphany was transferred in the west to the feast of the Nativity as well. On a famous occasion in 496 Clovis, King of the Franks and a very militant churchman, had his entire army baptized at Reims on Christmas Day along with himself.

* * * * *

In all these expositions, there was never a thought that the nativity of Jesus Christ was in any way independent of the cross and resurrection. The Fathers knew well enough that we have not been saved just by the events at Bethlehem. As Gregory of Nazianzus said in the passage just quoted, Christmas can be celebrated as a redemptive festival because we are 'born . . . crucified . . . buried . . . risen again with him.' Rightly understood, Christmas brings us to the one paschal mystery—the coming of man through Christ's death and resurrection into the life of God. The Orthodox call it 'another Easter.'

But Christmas did not immediately acquire the status of a second Pasch in the liturgical year. In a letter written about 400, Augustine pointed out that Easter was specially related to our salvation because the Christian has participated in it through his own baptismal death and resurrection in Christ.

[15] *Sermons*, p. 127.

It was 'a celebration which, commemorating a historical event, sets before our eyes the sign of the sacred reality which must be devoutly accepted.' He called it a *sacramentum*—what we would describe today as 'a sacramental.' [16]

Christmas, on the other hand, was only a *memoria*, a 'commemoration.' As a date it was certainly hallowed in that it was the one day in the year chosen by God for the birth of his Son. Men often choose dates, but sometimes for the wrong reason: 'God did not make his choice of day after the manner of those silly people who think that the fates of men are bound up with the position of the stars. Obviously, he was not made happy by the day on which he was born; but the day on which he deigned to be born was made a happy one by him.' [17] Yet this did not give it the status of Easter in Augustine's estimation.

Perhaps we encounter in his attitude the conservatism of the Church to innovation. When he wrote that letter, Christmas had probably not been known in north Africa for more than fifty years—Epiphany for even less time. The Bishop of Hippo, as the great teacher he was, saw all the benefits of keeping the newer feasts, but they were not like the scriptural observances which wove themselves in and out of the New Testament writings and the Church's soteriology.

With Pope Leo, however, it was different. He belonged to the next generation of Christian leaders and by then Christmas had become more venerable. Moreover, he brought to the liturgy a sacramental outlook that is one of his most valuable contributions to Christian spirituality. For him all the festivals were more than mere commemorations. Everything they signified was made present and effective in the lives of those who observed them with the Church. Since Christ's saving acts themselves transcended history, so the celebrations of those acts in the liturgical year bestowed the grace of each act—Leo called it the *vertu*—on the participants.[18]

In this sense Christmas was for Leo a *sacramentum salutis*, a phrase generally translated nowadays as 'a mystery of salvation': 'As the year rolls round, there recurs for us the *sacramentum salutis* which, promised from the beginning and

[16] *Ep.*, 55, PL, 33, 204.
[17] *Sermons*, p. 101.
[18] Leo's use of words is analysed in a table in M.-B. de Soos, *Le Mystère Liturgique d'apres S. Léon le Grand* (1958), pp. 129ff.

accomplished in the fulness of time, will endure for ever. On this day we are moved to lift up our hearts to adore the divine mystery, so that the Church may celebrate the effect of God's great gift with great joy.' [19]

The nativity of Christ could be spoken of as happening *today*, not only because the effects of that saving event are eternal, but also because the Church's cultus made them present for the worshipper (we might say that there was a 'real presence' of Christ's nativity in the celebration of Christmas). It is an interpretation of the liturgical calendar which we have already come across in the Cappadocian Fathers ('With the star we ran, with the magi we worshipped, with the shepherds we were enlightened') but Leo applied to it the logic of the western mind and endeavoured to differentiate between an individual's contemplation of Christ's birth in the ordinary course of daily devotion and his celebration of that event in the liturgy on December 25th:

'On all days and at all times, dearly beloved, does the birth of our Lord and Saviour from the Virgin mother occur to the thoughts of the faithful, who meditate on divine things, that the mind may be aroused to the acknowledgment of its Maker; and whether it be occupied in the groans of supplication, or in the shouting of praise, or in the offering of sacrifice, it may employ its spiritual insight on nothing more frequently and more trustingly than on the fact that God, the Son of God, begotten of the co-eternal Father, was also born by a human birth. But this nativity, which is to be adored in heaven and on earth, is suggested to us by no day more than this when, with the early light still shedding its rays on nature, there is borne in upon our senses the brightness of this wondrous mystery. For the angel Gabriel's converse with the astonished Mary and her conception by the Holy Ghost, as wondrously promised as believed, seem to recur not only to the memory but to the very eyes. For today the Maker of the world was born of a Virgin's womb, and he, who made all natures, became Son of her, whom he created. Today the Word of God appeared clothed in flesh, and That which had never been visible to human eyes began to be tangible to our

[19] NPNF, 12, 129. This is discussed by J. Gaillard in 'Noël: memoria ou mystère?' an essay in *La Maison-Dieu*, 59 (1959), pp. 37ff. This number of LMD contains a number of useful studies under the general title of 'Avent, Noël, Épiphanie.'

hands as well. Today the shepherds learnt from angels' voices that the Saviour was born in the substance of our flesh and soul.' [20]

So the Church at Christmas praises God for what he has done and is still doing for mankind in Christ. Anticipating Easter, the Churches echoes the chorus of angels heard by the shepherds and, vested with the priesthood of all creation, she gives voice to the joy of the universe at the renewal of all things in the Creator.

This cosmic view of the Christmas celebrations is not brought out much in the eucharistic liturgy of the western Church, though an old collect from a Ravenna rite sums it up picturesquely in terms of a salvation-spring for the world:

'The whole Church rejoices today, Almighty Father, for thine only Son, whom the prophets foretold, came into this world as dew upon the grass and made joy to spring up abundantly. Therefore the earth also sings her delight, for, watered by the rain from heaven, she offers wonderful gifts to her Redeemer.'

The Christmas homily of Maximus of Turin, quoted in the last chapter, contained Revelation 21: 5 ('Behold, I make all things new') on which the bishop commented, 'We must not be surprised if, in the birth of Christ, all things become new, because he whom the Virgin bore is himself such a new thing.'

It was in the east that the cosmic scope of the Nativity was expressed more readily. Ephraem wrote:

'The Father, who at the beginning created all things, has sent his Son to restore them and bring them back to their former state. In fact, he renewed the whole world which Adam, stripped of his youthfulness after his sin, had caused to fall into ruin. The Creator of all things became the Restorer. He gave them back their former beauty.' [21]

The hymns of the Armenian liturgy sang:

'Thy epiphany, O Lord, made the earth leap for joy. . . . The choir of shepherds on earth glorified thy all-saving advent.'

'Today, the Word who sits on the throne of glory with the Father became flesh, born of the holy Virgin, giving the universe the grace of adoption.'

[20] NPNF, 12, p. 137.
[21] Quoted in Lemarié, p. 222.

46

IV. *Epiphany*

'Light of lights, thou hast appeared, O Christ, thou to whom the magi offered their gifts. Alleluia.'

This old antiphon, still used at Epiphany in the Roman Church, breathes the original spirit of the feast. God is manifested in Christ as a light for all peoples. Gregory of Nazianzus called January 6th 'the day of holy lights.' Another unknown homilist spoke of Christ on this day as 'the bringer of more light than any "Sun" day.' Like the primitive Christmas, the primitive Epiphany was a celebration of Christ's *appearing*. Even in the Mozarabic calendar it was called the feast of the *Apparitio Domini*—a title it shared in some service books with December 25th, illustrating the early similarity between the two festivals. It was only when Christmas was kept in the Churches along with Epiphany that December 25th came to be associated exclusively with the birth at Bethlehem and January 6th with the adoration of the magi, the baptism in the river Jordan, and the wedding at Cana—though with different emphases in east and west, as we shall see in a moment.

This evolution in the feasts concentrated the Church's attention at Epiphany on those preliminary episodes in the Gospel narratives which manifested God's glory in the life of Christ. As a celebration of God's *manifestio* and Christ's *apparitio*, Epiphany is still nearer the intention of the early Christian midwinter festivals than Christmas has since become. It contains the Church's response to hopes expressed in the ancient worship of *Sol*. For the Christian, the Saviour is no distant deity, making himself known only in the shadowy signs of Dionysius or the mysterious rites of Mithras. He is present in Christ in the fullness of his divine nature. Manifested in the flesh, God has revealed himself to man in the person of a perfect man, through whom all mankind may be united eternally with him.

In this conviction, the Fathers expounded the details of the magi story as indications of Christ's divinity—minor theophanies through which the initiated can read the truths of God's redeeming work. The star was a particularly evocative symbol. Variously interpreted as a figure of an angel or as a sign of the Holy Spirit, it pointed the magi (and so also the members of the Church who meditate on the Gospel) to Christ.

'Is it to be wondered at,' asked John Chrysostom, 'that a divine star ministers to the rising Sun of Righteousness? It halts above the head of the Child as if saying, "This is he." '

Similarly Ambrose said:

'The star is seen by the magi; where Herod is, it is not seen; it is seen again where Christ is, and shows them the way. Therefore this star is the way, and the way is Christ: for in the mystery of the incarnation Christ is a star. "A star shall rise out of Jacob, and a man shall rise up from Israel." So where Christ is, the star is. For he himself is "the bright and morning star." He shows us himself by his own light.' [1]

The oracle of Balaam, quoted here by Ambrose, recalled that in the east the star was a symbol of kingship—the star of David—and with the magi's question, 'Where is he that is born King of the Jews?' the homilists treated Epiphany as a festival of Christ's Kingdom.

The magi's gifts were also interpreted in the same way. Leo is only one of the multitude of preachers who have pointed out their familiar significance:

'The magi . . . adore the Word in our flesh, Wisdom in infancy, Power in weakness, and in true man the Lord of majesty. And that they may make clear the mystery of their faith and understanding, they proclaim by their gifts that which they believe in their hearts. They offer incense to God, myrrh to man, and gold to a King.' [2]

In the east Basil had said much the same thing, but with an allegorical exegesis of Numbers 24 typical of the Fathers:

'Without doubt the magi fulfilled the prophecy of Balaam, who said about Christ, "He crouched, he lay down like a lion and a lioness; who will rouse him up? Blessed be everyone who blesses you, and cursed be everyone who curses you." By "lion" scripture refers to royal dignity; by "lay down" to the passion; and by the power of blessing to the divinity. In

---

[1] Toal, pp. 222, 213.
[2] Ibid., p. 227.

fulfilling this prophecy, the magi offered gold as to a king, myrrh as to a mortal man, and incense as to God.'[3]

The meaning of the gifts was not always explained in this familiar way. John Chrysostom saw both the incense and the gold as indications of Christ's divinity:

'But what was it that moved the magi to adore him? For the Virgin bore upon her no distinguishing mark, and the abode was not one of splendour; neither was there any other material circumstance which would either compel them or induce them to do this. Yet not alone do they adore him, but opening their treasures they offer him gifts; and such gifts as are offered, not to man, but to God. For gold and incense especially were a symbol of the divinity. What then was it that moved them? It was that which had before moved them, so that leaving their own country they had begun this weary journey, namely: the star, together with the light that God had placed in their hearts, which was to lead them step by step to more perfect knowledge.'[4]

Ephraem's interpretation was more fanciful: he inferred that the gold represented the idols of the heathen, given back to the true God, while the myrrh and incense represented the medicine brought by the heavenly Doctor to heal the wounds of Adam!

The authors of the Armenian liturgy perceived in the number of the gifts a reflection of the *Trisagion* worship of the seraphim. Like the unending *Holy, Holy, Holy* of the angelic chorus, the gold, the incense and the myrrh constitute the homage of the Church militant to the Blessed Trinity:

'Thou who art praised unceasingly by the creatures with four faces in the song of the *Trisagion*, thou hast been honoured by the magi's gifts in the manger.'

The association of Psalm 72 with the event—'The kings of Tharsis and of the isles shall give presents: the kings of Arabia and Saba shall bring gifts'—has influenced Christian traditions so that in later ages the magi were depicted in liturgical devotion and drama as three kings. But neither in the works of the Fathers nor in early Christian art are they represented as being anything other than wise men. (The one exception to this is a single reference in Tertullian where he speaks of them as kings.)

[3] Quoted in Lemarié, p. 244.
[4] Toal, p. 215.

49

D

Allegorically, the magi are the hosts of non-Jewish peoples who have been brought into the presence of God in Christ—the Church of the Gentiles. 'He who was last, the Gentile, became the first,' said Peter Chrysologus, Bishop of Ravenna (*d. c.* 450). 'From the faith of the magi the belief of the Gentiles was inaugurated and the cruelty of the Jews made manifest.' [5]

The hostility of Herod and the Jews prefigured the future rejection of the Saviour by his own people. Maximus of Turin mused on the significance of the fact that the magi came from the lands on which the sun rose first in the morning while the Jews came from Egypt: 'The Gentiles, all enlightened, came from the east; but Judah, blinded by unbelief which hardened their hearts, came from the west. The Jews mistook the presence of the Sun who never slept; they lost the day that never ends.' [6]

The comparative novelty of Epiphany in the west in Augustine's time is shown by the way he had to explain to his Latin congregation that the title of the feast meant *manifestio* in their language. It was, he pointed out, a particularly appropriate celebration for them as members of the Gentile Church:

'The magi came from the east to adore the newborn Child of the Virgin. We celebrate this day today with all due solemnity and a sermon. That first day dawned upon them; it has returned to us on its yearly feast. They were the first-fruits of the Gentiles; we are the people of the Gentiles.'

The two feasts of Christmas and Epiphany were like the two sides of an arch, he said, coining Paul's image; they represent the Jewish and the Gentile inheritance under the new covenant:

'Only a few days ago we celebrated the Lord's birthday. Today we are celebrating with equal solemnity, as is proper, his Epiphany, in which he began to manifest himself to the Gentiles. On the one day the Jewish shepherds saw him when he was born; on this day the magi coming from the east adored him. Now, he had been born that Cornerstone, the peace of the two walls coming from very different directions, from circumcision and uncircumcision. Thus they could be united in him who had been made our peace, and "who has made both one." This was foretokened in the Jewish shep-

[5] PL, 52, 621.
[6] PL, 57, 282.

herds and the Gentile magi. From this began what was to grow and to bear fruit throughout the world. Let us, therefore, with joy of the spirit hold dear these two days, the Nativity and the Manifestation of our Lord. The Jewish shepherds were led to him by an angel bringing the news; the Gentile magi by a star showing the way.' [7]

The Church is a city enlightened by the manifestation of God in Christ. In the introit for the mass of the Epiphany in the Milanese rite, the compilers drew on Revelation 12: 'The city has no need of the light of the sun and that of the moon: for the light of God illuminates it and all nations walk by its light.' And in the collect for the vigil of the feast, the Gelasian Sacramentary, which contains some of the earliest liturgical texts of the Church in Rome, prays that the Epiphany light may enable God's people to know and comprehend the divine truth:

'Make thy light to shine upon thy people, we beseech thee, O Lord, and from the splendour of thy grace enlighten our hearts, so that thy people may know the Saviour for ever and understand him in all truth.'

The final episode in the infancy narrative, the flight into Egypt, John Chrysostom saw as a blessing by God on that land: 'In going there he sanctified the whole country.' The results of that blessing, he went on, were to be seen in the ascetics of the desert. By the fourth century, Egyptian monasticism was in its heyday—in the upper Nile basin alone there were nearly five hundred settlements with their attendant monasteries.

'Should you now enter the desert land of Egypt,' he said, 'you will find the solitudes more wonderful than any paradise, thousands of choirs of angels in human form, nations of martyrs, hosts of virgins, the whole evil dominion of the demon cast down, the kingdom of Christ resplendent. . . . Heaven itself with all the splendour of the stars is not as splendid as the solitudes of Egypt, which spread out before us in every direction the dwelling places of her contemplatives.' [8]

Archaeologists have recovered early representations of the

---

[7] *Sermons,* p. 164.
[8] Toal, p. 219. Jerome was less enthusiastic. When he came from Rome to the desert of Syria in 373 he complained that it was too crowded!

Epiphany in ampullas, frescoes and ivories, showing the Virgin Mary enthroned and presenting the Holy Child in her arms to the world. There is a fine example in an ivory from Jordan in the British Museum: on either side of the Virgin the three magi offer their gifts and an angel, holding a staff with a cross, completes the group. The lesson of January 6th is simply but vividly portrayed for all to learn.

＊　　＊　　＊　　＊　　＊

There are texts in the western rites which refer to the baptism in the Jordan and the wedding at Cana on the feast of Epiphany, but the trend in the Roman missal was to relate these events to days after the festival. It is only Gallican lectionaries like Luxeuil and Bobbio which set these readings for January 6th—faithful, as usual, to the traditions of the eastern Churches. G. G. Willis' reconstructions of the lectionaries used by Augustine, Peter Chrysologus, Maximus and Leo all show that Matthew 2 was the gospel for that day.[9] For patristic and liturgical material associated with the themes of the baptism in the Jordan and the wedding at Cana on the feast of the Epiphany, therefore, we shall have to rely largely on texts from the east.

The baptism in the Jordan was (and still is) associated with the feast in eastern Christendom because the public ministry of Christ was initiated by this *epiphania*. Indeed, in the traditions followed by St. Mark and St. John, it is the first manifestation of God in the Gospel. So the details of the scriptural passages were utilized to teach congregations that the baptism was a theophany of the three Persons of the Trinity. The voice from heaven declaring 'This is my beloved Son' revealed the eternal generation of the Second Person of the Trinity from the Father, and the appearance of the Holy Spirit in the form of a dove authenticated and sealed that declaration.

Severian, Bishop of Gabala (*fl. c.* 400), John Chrysostom's opponent at Constantinople, said in a homily for the Theophany:

'The adorable Trinity is present in all glory: the Father from on high proclaims his Son; the Son on earth accom-

<hr>

[9] *St. Augustine's Lectionary* (1962), pp. 94ff.

plishes the economy of salvation; the Holy Spirit certifies by his seal the divine initiative.'

An unknown preacher in north Africa of about the same period said much the same thing:

'In the baptism I see not only a witness to Christ. I also see there a mystery of the Trinity. Because the whole Godhead proclaimed the Saviour as the only-begotten Son of God, the divine Persons manifested themselves in three ways.' [10]

It is possible that in some parts of north Africa the feast of the Epiphany was known as 'the day of the Trinity'—at least, it is referred to in these terms in another anonymous homily.

In their characteristic way, the eastern liturgies highlighted the theological significance of the event by quasi-dramatic comments by the characters concerned, drawing freely from scriptural material. A chant in the Byzantine rite for terce on the feast expresses the reaction of John the Baptist to Christ's request for baptism:

'The right hand of the Forerunner, the Baptist, the Prophet most honoured of all prophets, began trembling when he saw thee, the Lamb of God that taketh away the sins of the world; and in distress he cried out to thee: 'I dare not touch thy head, O Word; O most merciful, sanctify me and enlighten me, for thou art the life and the light and the peace of the world!' '

Another chant quaintly described the astonishment of the angels as they watched the proceedings:

'The choirs of angels, seeing the invisible One coming through the waters, were seized with awe, that the invisible God could have taken the form of a servant. His epiphany gave light to the world. Blessed art thou, Lord God of Israel!' '

In the Lucan narrative Jesus returns to Galilee after his baptism and temptations in the wilderness and preaches in the synagogue at Nazareth on verses from Isaiah 61 ('The Spirit of the Lord is upon me, because he has anointed me . . . '). When did the Spirit descend and anoint him? asked the homilists: surely, in the Jordan! From this Chrysostom explained that Christ is the Temple of God, washed and anointed by the Holy Spirit—the Temple that was destroyed to be raised again in three days. Eastern chants in Epiphany

[10] Quoted in Lemarié, p. 289.

rites referred to Jesus as 'the newly-built Temple of God' while in some lectionaries the story of Aaron's consecration by Moses (Leviticus 8: 1–13) was read on the feast as a 'type' or prefiguring of the baptism in Jordan.

Another expository theme was drawn from the philology of Aramaic in which the word for 'lamb' is the same as that for 'servant.' John the Baptist's heralding of Christ could be read: 'Behold, the Servant of God, who takes away the sin of the world.' And this in turn recalled the prophecy of Isaiah: 'Behold, my Servant. . . . I have put my Spirit upon him.' So the baptism in Jordan was understood as the moment when Christ entered the ring against Satan and, full of the Spirit, went out into the wilderness to meet his adversary. It corresponded with the entry into Jerusalem as a further move by God in the war against evil, and a hymn of the Armenian rite links these two entrances by joining the shouts of Palm Sunday to the baptism in the Jordan:

'He was baptized in Jordan under the eyes of the Father and of the Spirit. Hosanna in the highest, sing the children. Blessings to the Son of David.'

Because the liturgy celebrates events from a post-paschal perspective, the Church saw in the baptism an epiphany of Christ's triumph. In scriptural thought, water symbolizes (among other things) the abode of evil. According to one tradition, which can be charted through the Psalms, Job and Isaiah, Yahweh trampled on the mythical monsters of the deep, Leviathian and Rahab, the figures of evil and chaos. Stepping down into the river, therefore, Christ at his baptism stamped out the power of the devil. This is why in the oriental rites, Psalm 74 is often associated with the Epiphany: 'Thou didst divide the sea through thy power: thou breakest the heads of the dragons in the waters.'

The baptism in the Jordan prefigured Christ's descent into hell. As the Christian at his initiation is joined to our Lord's death and resurrection, the Saviour's baptism looked forward to his own death on the cross and his journey to the place of the departed spirits before his triumphant resurrection. Another chant expressed it this way:

'You have descended to earth to save Adam, O Lord, and, not finding him there, you have gone down into hell to search him out.'

Contemplating Christ's baptism, the Church came to realize

more clearly the significance of her own. Jordan was the font. 'Christ submitted to be cleansed in the Jordan for my purification,' said Gregory of Nazianzus. 'Or, rather, he sanctified the waters by his purification.'

'The living waters of the incarnate Word came to Jordan,' preached Severus of Antioch on the festival. 'This is why the Lord said, "I have made these waters pure and henceforth death will not exist." When the living waters had been mixed with the Jordan, they bruised the head of the dragon who, according to David, had brought about the death of Adam by his wicked counsel.' [11]

The saving events in Israel's history connected with water were summoned to illustrate the significance of Christ's baptism. By sending the Holy Spirit in the form of a dove on Jesus as he stepped from the river, the Father had introduced the new Noah launching the ark of salvation, the Church. Formerly God had led his people through the sea by the pillars of cloud and of fire, now he was leading them himself through the waters of baptism. The Saviour was another Joshua, taking his people over the Jordan to capture the promised land. The flame that had consumed the sacrifice offered by Elijah on Mount Carmel now spread as a living fire in the baptismal waters. Christ drove back the demons as Elisha, with Elijah's mantle, parted the waters. . . . Thus the images succeeded one another in a fantastic galaxy of allegory and reinterpretation.

Behind it is the Byzantine Church's practice of administering the sacrament of initiation on the festival. Another name for baptism was *hō phōtismos*, 'the illumination,' and the feast of Lights was chosen as a fitting time to bring catechumens to baptismal enlightenment. Like the western texts which associated Christmas with a Christian's adoption as a son of God, the Epiphany rites also refer to man's life in the Church. The Gothic missal, one of the most important sources for the early Gallican liturgy, has an Epiphany preface which draws these themes together:

'From the heavens over Jordan's bed the thunder rolled, telling us that you were there; it showed us the Saviour, who had come to us from heaven; it showed us you, the Father of

[11] From the French translation in *Patrologia Orientalis,* 23 (1907ff.), pp. 30–1.

the eternal Light. You opened the heavens, blessed the air and cleansed the waters, and through the Holy Spirit, who appeared like a dove, you showed us your only Son. This was the day when the waters received your blessing and took away the curse that had been laid on us. Now they can wash all sins away, if only men will believe; now they can make new children for God, adopting them to eternal life. Our birth in the flesh destined us to a life in time, our sin made us the prisoners of death; but now eternal life is open to us and we are called back to glory in the kingdom of heaven.' [12]

Since Christ's baptism is also the baptism of the Church, it was surrounded with the concept of the holy marriage in Ephesians 5: 25–7: 'Christ loved the Church and gave himself up for her, that he might sanctify her, having cleansed her by the washing of water with the word, that he might present the Church to himself in splendour, without spot or wrinkle or any such thing, that she might be holy and without blemish.' Pre-nuptial baths were an important feature of oriental wedding ceremonies, and the Syrian rites hailed the baptism in the Jordan in these terms, seeing John the Baptist in the role of the Bridegroom's friend:

'Glory be to thee, spiritual Bridegroom, who prepared the fulness of joy for your Bride when you espoused her from among mortal men; and who celebrated a wonderful marriage feast in her honour in the river Jordan when, in your love, you came up from among the multitudes of Judah to be baptized by your servant.'

The blessing of waters on the feast of the Epiphany is thought by some to be a Christian version of a pagan ceremony, by others to be a pre-baptismal blessing. Various prayers are used in different rites:

'This day the heavens were opened, and the sea was made sweet: the earth rejoices and the mountains and hills are glad, because Christ is baptized of John in Jordan';

'The voice of the Lord crieth upon the waters, saying, "O come ye and receive ye all the Spirit of wisdom, the Spirit of understanding, the Spirit of the fear of God, even Christ, who is made manifest." '

A Syriac rubric instructs the archimandrite and his attendant priests to wave a fan over 'the fountain, or the well, or

[12] Preface for the Epiphany, quoted in A. Hamman, *Early Christian Prayers* (Eng. tr. 1961), p. 248.

the pool, or the river,' to symbolize the breath of the Holy Spirit! [13]

*   *   *   *   *

'Christ the Bridegroom, having been baptized, he could open the splendid doors of the heavenly bridal chamber.'

Another ancient antiphon leads us to the third theme of Epiphany, the marriage at Cana. A certain mystery surrounds the original connection of this episode with Epiphany. It may have been the association of the holy-marriage-concept with God's manifestation in flesh, or it may have been the Church's response to the water-into-wine myths current in pagan mythology on January 6th. Anyway, the miracle is read either on the feast itself or a few days afterwards in the liturgical tradition of the Church, and consequently it was the subject of sermons.

'Let us try to understand the mystical meaning of the miracle,' said Peter Chrysologus. 'What do they represent—these nuptials, celebrated with the Saviour's assistance? Surely they are a figure of those nuptials by which Christ unites himself to the Church: for like a bridegroom coming forth out of his chamber, he approaches his beloved with a covenant of promise; and then he set to work: with water he made wine—that is, with the Gentiles he made his faithful people.' [14]

Cyril of Alexandria pointed out that the marriage at Cana took place 'on the third day' (John 2: 1) and expounded the inner meaning of the phrase as another sign of the new age manifested by the miracle:

' "The third day" is the last age of the world, for the number 3 signifies for us a beginning, a middle and an end. . . . This is borne out by the prophet, "He will strike and he will cure us. He will revive us after two days: on the third day he will raise us up, and we shall live in his sight. We shall know, and we shall follow on, that we may know the Lord. His

[13] These quotations are from *The Blessing of the Waters on the Eve of the Epiphany,* ed. by John, Marquess of Bute and E. A. Wallis Budge (1901). The sixth century pilgrim to the Holy Land was taken to the Place of Baptism on the river Jordan, as he still is today, to see the ceremony—which includes the dipping of a cross into the water.

[14] Quoted in Lemarié, p. 402.

going forth is prepared in the morning light!" . . . On the third day he healed those who were stricken with corruption and death. Not in the first age, nor in the middle, but in these last times, when, becoming man, he restored all human nature, raising it in himself from the dead. And so he is called "the firstfruits of them that sleep." Therefore when the evangelist speaks of "the third day," on which was celebrated the wedding feast, he means this present age.' [15]

The Gothic missal has a preface for Epiphany which uses the miracle at Cana as a reason for calling on God to consecrate the elements in the eucharistic chalice:

'We beseech the Lord, who changed water into wine, to change the wine which we offer into his Blood, and we pray that he, who always gives his guests abundant drink, may sanctify us by the libation of his Cup and the infusion of the Holy Ghost the Comforter.'

Another Johannine sign, the multiplication of the loaves, was also sometimes referred to at Epiphanytide as a eucharistic symbol:

'Almighty God, who hast manifested thyself this day by the miraculous sign, changing water into wine and multiplying the loaves in the baskets, . . . fill thy faithful people with the wine of righteousness and grant them to participate in this banquet. . . . ' [16]

So Epiphany became a 'second Easter'—a celebration of the total content of redemption in Jesus Christ through his Church. Christian homiletic and liturgical sources boldly seized the scriptural passages which have been misrepresented by heretical sects of every age—adoptionists have always quoted the baptism in the Jordan as a justification for their tenets (the Jehovah's Witnesses still do today)—and set them within the advent of God for the salvation of the world. And they did this with an inspired discernment and a spiritual zest that we can feel in the texts as they have survived down to our own times.

What we have inherited from them in the west is in the Roman missal and the Prayer Book and its successors.

[15] Toal, p. 277.
[16] *Missale Gothicum,* ed. H. M. Bannister (Henry Bradshaw Society, 52), p. 26.

V. The Liturgy of the Feasts

"Because by divine provision we celebrate the mysteries of the mass three times today, we are not able to speak at length on the gospel reading.'

This casual remark at the beginning of one of Gregory the Great's Christmas homilies indicates that during his pontificate (590–604) the feast was kept in Rome with three masses—the three sets of formularies for Christmas (the midnight mass, the mass at dawn, and the mass of the day) are, of course, a familiar feature of the Roman missal. But when December 25th was first observed in the liturgical calendar as the *natale Domini,* there could only have been one mass. What were its formularies? [1]

G. G. Willis has shown that in many parts of Italy, Gaul, Spain and North Africa, Luke 2 was commonly read on Christmas Day. In Rome, however, Matthew 2, the adoration of the magi, may have been the most primitive gospel of the day. The evidence for this has recently been discussed by C. Coebergh, and the points he makes are these.

First, Roman iconography in the fourth and the first half

[1] For readers who may not be familiar with the Roman missal, I should explain that the formularies for each mass usually consist of at least three prayers (collect, secret, postcommunion), two readings (epistle, gospel) and a series of chants. The secret is said after the offertory and the postcommunion at the end of the service. The chants are the relics of days when psalms or passages of scripture were sung at various points in the mass—the introit with its antiphon at the entrance of the clergy, the gradual and the alleluia with its verse between the readings, the offertory when the bread and wine and offerings are brought to the holy table, and the communion as the celebrant and the congregation are receiving the sacrament. For a discussion of the origins of these formularies, see J. A. Jungmann, *The Mass of the Roman Rite* (Eng. tr. 1959). In this and the following chapter I have quoted from *The English Missal* (Anglican, published by W. Knott & Son, Ltd.) and *The Saint Andrew Daily Missal* (Roman, published by the Abbey of St. Andrew, Bruges). For simplicity I have used the term 'epistle' to denote the first reading at the eucharist, even when the pericope is taken from Acts or from the Old Testament.

of the fifth century always depicts the adoration of the magi when the subject is the nativity of our Lord. There are many similar examples among the frescoes in Rome and the seventeen sarcophagi exhibited in the Lateran museum are all decorated with the same motif. Furthermore, when Sixtus III (432–440) had the Liberian basilica rebuilt and dedicated in honour of the Virgin Mary (the present St. Mary Major) the mosaic over the apse was executed to show the magi's visit.

Second, in the east the adoration of the magi was one of the epiphanies celebrated when the Church kept January 6th as a feast of Christ's nativity. The Armenian lectionary provides Matthew 2 as the lesson for the eucharist on that day.

Third, the adoration of the magi is given some prominence in the Nativity sermons and readings in other early sources. The first known Christmas homily, that of Optatus of Milevis, speaks of the intrigues of Herod and the gifts of the magi. The sermons of Severus reveal that Matthew 2 was the gospel lesson on December 25th. A Byzantine *typicon*, or liturgical manual, in a tenth century manuscript which preserves earlier usage, gives the magi's visit as the gospel for Christmas Day, and the Bobbio Missal similarly sets Matthew 2 as the Christmas reading.

Finally, there is the position of the feast of Holy Innocents in the Roman calendar. This has occupied December 28th from very early times. If the story of the visit of the magi had been read on Christmas Day, we would expect the account of the consequences of that visit, the murder of the children, to be read soon afterwards—bearing in mind that a continuous reading of scripture (*lectio continua*) was usual before the lectionaries were drawn up.[2]

When Epiphany was observed in Rome, however, Matthew 2 was transferred to January 6th and the Lucan infancy narrative came to be read on Christmas Day.

But why were three masses provided by the end of the sixth century?

Early in the fifth century, the eucharist was celebrated at dawn on Christmas Day in St. Peter's after a vigil office *ad gallicantum*. If Fr. Coebergh's arguments are correct, this had a gospel lesson from Matthew, later to be changed to

[2] C. Coebergh, 'Les pericopes d'évangile de la fête de Noël à Rome' in *Revue Bénédictine*, 76 (1966), pp. 128ff.

Luke 2. It is not known what the epistle was. It may have been the pericope from Hebrews which now appears in the mass of the day in the missal and as the Christmas epistle in the Prayer Book.

During the next hundred years, the liturgical experiments of the Church in Jerusalem exercised a powerful influence over the worship of Christians in Rome and elsewhere. From accounts by pilgrims like Egeria and scholars like Jerome, the historical-commemorative ethos of the Jerusalem celebrations, resulting from services in and around the churches built over the Holy Places, began to affect the local calendars. There was an urge to do things at home as they were done in Jerusalem, and congregations began to keep the anniversaries of the saving events in the life of our Lord in a more elaborate liturgical year.

Consequently, some time during the fifth century the eucharist celebrated in Bethlehem for the Nativity of Christ on the night of January 5th–6th was copied in Rome with a midnight mass in St. Peter's on Christmas eve. The gospel was Luke 2, perhaps ending at verse 20, 'And the shepherds returned, glorifying and praising God for all the things that they had heard and seen, as it was told unto them.' The mass was celebrated at about the hour the event occurred. But the epistle from Titus 2—almost certainly the same pericope as that used for the eucharist at Bethlehem, for it is the reading always set for Epiphany in the eastern rites—also gave the celebration its special character as an occasion of rejoicing for God's manifestation in Christ's coming and appearing. This is brought out strikingly if we print the Greek and Latin versions of two words in the passage: 'The grace of God that bringeth salvation hath appeared (*epiphane, apparuit*) to all men . . . looking for that blessed hope, and the appearing (*epiphaneian, adventum*) of our great God and Saviour Jesus Christ.'

Psalm 2 was chosen for the introit, but when sacristies were built in the Roman basilicas nearer the altar, the entrance of the sanctuary party took less time and the length of the introit was cut down. As was often the case, only the first verse was used: 'Why do the heathen so furiously rage together: and why do the people imagine a vain thing?' It is hardly appropriate by itself for Christmas Day. The antiphon to the introit, however, has retained the key verse of the psalm, showing why it was originally chosen: 'Thou art my Son, this day have I begotten thee.' It was also used as the verse for the alleluia. The gradual and communion sentence are from the Latin version of Psalm 110: 'I begot thee from the womb before the day star.' The offertory from Psalm 96 echoes the joy of the feast: 'Let the heavens rejoice, and let the earth be glad before the Lord: for he is come.' The collect was specially composed for the mass: it speaks of 'this most sacred night' being made 'to shine with the brightness of true light' and 'the mysteries of this light on earth.'

The midnight mass was eventually transferred in Rome from St. Peter's to St. Mary Major, where a chapel had been built modelled on the grotto of the nativity at Bethlehem. The missal still carries the notice that the station of this mass is St. Mary Major *ad praesepe* 'at the manger' which, in the chapel, formed the altar.[3]

When the pope began celebrating the Christmas mass at midnight, the morning service was for a while presided over by a priest and then dropped altogether. But John III (561–574) instituted a second mass at the *titulus Anastasiae*, a church on the north side of the Aventine for the court of the Byzantine governor, set up in Rome by Justinian after the conquest of Italy in the middle of the sixth century. This old church was quite close to the homes of the Byzantine officials.

Who Anastasia was is not known. It is probable that she was a pious soul who, in the early days of the Roman Church, bequeathed her property to the Christian community and whose name attached itself to the church which was eventually built on the site. Several of the oldest churches in the city acquired their dedications in this way. But it so happened that a famous fourth century martyr of Sirmium (Mitrowitz in Yugoslavia), highly honoured by Byzantine Christians, was also called Anastasia and her *natale* in the Roman calendar was December 25th. This series of coincidences resulted in the pope personally celebrating mass for the Byzantine court in St. Anastasia on Christmas Day. The Gregorian Sacramentary provides a collect, a secret, a preface and a postcommunion commemorating the saint *before* the formularies for the feast of the *Apparitio Domini*.

After the Byzantine hegemony had ended, the tradition of

[3] See p. 104 below. The 'station' was the church where the pope said mass on particular occasions.

a papal mass early on Christmas morning at this particular church was so well established that it became part of the programme in the Roman liturgy for the day. The missal still designates St. Anastasia as the stational church for this mass and includes a commemoration of the saint along with the other prayers. Such is the origin of the Christmas mass 'at dawn' (*in aurora*).

The present lessons and chants may be original. The epistle and the gospel (Titus 3:4–7 and Luke 2:15–20) look as if they have been borrowed from the last verses of the midnight readings. Like the midnight epistle, the dawn epistle begins with the Christmas leitmotif, *Apparuit,* and introduces the themes of salvation, baptism and renewal: 'He saved us by the washing of regeneration and renewing of the Holy Ghost, which he shed on us abundantly through Jesus Christ our Saviour'; the gospel tells how the shepherds went to Bethlehem in response to the heavenly vision and then returned glorifying and praising God.

The chants spin out the themes of dawning light and of the advent of the divine ruler: 'Light shall shine upon us today: for unto us the Lord is born: and he shall be called Wonderful, God, the Prince of Peace, Father of the world to come: of whose kingdom there shall be no end. The Lord is king, and hath put on glorious apparel: the Lord hath put on his apparel, and girded himself with strength' (antiphon and introit, alleluia verse); 'Blessed is he that cometh in the name of the Lord: God is the Lord who hath shewed us light. This is the Lord's doing: and it is marvellous in our eyes' (gradual); 'God hath made the round world so sure, that it cannot be moved: ever since the world began, hath thy seat, O God, been prepared, thou art from everlasting' (offertory); 'Rejoice greatly, O daughter of Zion, shout, O daughter of Jerusalem: behold, thy king cometh, the holy one and the Saviour of the world' (communion). These are all traditionally associated with the feast in different rites. Egeria tells us that verses 26 and 27 ('God is the Lord who hath shewed us light . . . ') were chanted over and over again by the pilgrims as they went in procession with the Bishop back to Jerusalem after the nocturnal eucharist at Bethlehem. But was a special emphasis placed on the theme of Christ the King in Rome at this mass because it was first celebrated for those who belonged to the ruling circles in the Byzantine empire?

63

The third mass of the day was celebrated in St. Peter's until it was transferred to St. Mary Major in the twelfth century. It has the prologue of John as its gospel and Hebrews 1: 1–12 as its epistle, making the celebration what L. Baumstark calls 'a feast of the Nicene Dogma.' The gospel is one of the key passages in scripture for the doctrine of the Incarnation, moving from the creation achieved by the Word of God to the recreation accomplished by the Word made flesh (though some have pointed out that this reading would be better if it were continued to verse 16 to include the reference to Christ's redeeming work in us: 'And of his fulness have all we received, and grace for grace'). The epistle in some respects follows the same movement of thought as the gospel. It mentions Christ's work on earth and describes his enthronement in heaven; it points out his supremacy over all the ancient prophets and his relationship to the angels (superior in that he is divine, inferior in that he became what an angel can never be, a real man of flesh and blood); and it supports this assertion by quoting a series of *testimonia* from the Old Testament. There is a forceful anti-heresy intention behind the selection of both passages. Arianism, with its denial of Christ's Godhead, flourished in the west under the Gothic kings.

The liturgical texts have preserved the Old Latin translation of Isaiah 9, which is used for the introit antiphon: 'Unto us a child is born, unto us a son is given: the government shall be upon his shoulder, and his name shall be called, Angel of mighty counsel.' [4] The idea of the *Christos Angelos* was extremely popular in the early centuries until its limitations were recognized in the cross-currents of heretical teachings.

The introit itself, the gradual and the communion are all verses of Psalm 98, 'O sing unto the Lord a new song: for he hath done marvellous things' and 'All the ends of the world have seen the salvation of our God,' while the offertory comes from Psalm 89, recalling the creative office of the Word of God, 'The heavens are thine, the earth also is thine: thou hast laid the foundation of the round world, and all that therein is: righteousness and equity are the habitation of thy

[4] *Magni consilii angelus* instead of the more familiar *consiliarius*. For this information I am indebted to the publisher's reader, who very kindly made a number of helpful suggestions when this book was in the manuscript stage of production.

seat.' The alleluia verse is an amalgam of scriptural phrases, hinged on the solar symbolism of the feast: 'Alleluia, alleluia. A hallowed day hath dawned upon us: come, ye nations, and worship the Lord: for on this day a great light hath descended upon the earth. Alleluia.'

Among the prayers in the missal, the *communicantes* is certainly very ancient ('celebrating the most sacred night whereon the undefiled virginity of the blessed Mary brought forth the Saviour of the world') and the postcommunion of the third mass ('Grant, we beseech thee, Almighty God, that as he who was born this day is the author of our heavenly birth, so he may likewise bestow on us the gift of everlasting life') is the only collect for Christmas Day in the Gelasian sacramentary. Other collects bear traces of Leo's concept of Christmas as a *sacramentum salutis* ('O Lord, who by the wondrous birth of thy Son hast put away the old nature of our manhood, grant that by this sacrament of thy Nativity we may be restored unto newness of life'—postcommunion, second mass). They celebrate Christ's birth as a day of regeneration and renewal in the life of the Christian. *Nova nativitas* is, as we have seen, a major theme of the Christmas proclamation.

*   *   *   *   *

By the time the formularies for Epiphany had been assembled in the Roman missal, that day had become in the west a commemoration of the visit of the magi and all that that event implied. The gospel is Matthew 2: 1–12, the story of the magi, their interview with Herod and their presentation of the gifts. From the sixth century, if not earlier, the epistle has been Isaiah 60: 1–6, 'Arise, shine; for your light has come, and the glory of the Lord has risen upon you.' The prophecy is addressed to Jerusalem—inspired, no doubt, by the sight which every pilgrim sees when he watches the sunrise from the Mount of Olives. The Holy City is a figure of the Church: 'Nations shall come to your light, and kings to the brightness of your rising.'

The minds of the worshippers are directed towards the symbolism of the magi's visit as they sing in the gradual the key verse taken from the lesson: 'All they from Saba shall come, bringing gold and incense, and shall shew forth the praises of the Lord.' Then in the alleluia verse they prepare

65

to listen to the well-known story by chanting its most familiar words: 'We have seen his star in the east: and are come with gifts to worship the Lord.' This, of course, is what the congregation itself is also doing at the eucharist—coming with gifts to worship God. These chants are models of the way in which scriptural material can be used by the congregation to contemplate and to respond to the mystery celebrated in the liturgy. There are few hymns in use today which fulfil this role so fittingly.

Unfortunately, the effect is spoilt by the introit. At one time the whole of Psalm 72 was sung, because of its appropriate verses ten and eleven: 'The kings of Tharsis and of the isles shall give presents: the kings of Arabia and Saba shall bring gifts.' Then, when the introit was shortened to one verse, only the first verse was retained, and—as in the introit at Christmas—it is not particularly suitable: 'Give the king thy judgements, O God: and thy righteousness unto the king's son.' The antiphon from Malachi 3, however, is better: 'Behold, the Lord the ruler is come: and in his hand the kingdom, the power, and the dominion.' The communion sentence repeats the magi's greeting.

The secret was borrowed from Gaul: 'We beseech thee, O Lord, mercifully to look on the gifts of thy Church: by which we do not offer thee gold, frankincense and myrrh, but that which is signified, immolated and received by these gifts, Jesus Christ, thy Son, our Lord.' It makes an interesting bridge between the ministry of the Word and the ministry of the Sacrament. The old *oratio* for the day is now the collect for January 13th, the octave of Epiphany before the recent revisions in the Roman rite. It echoes the ancient character of the feast: 'O God, whose only begotten Son hath been manifest in the substance of our flesh. . . . ' The present collect was probably composed by Gregory the Great—by which time the western Church had set the visit of the magi into the centre of the Epiphany celebration: 'O God, who by the leading of a star didst manifest thy only begotten Son to the Gentiles. . . . '

Although the formularies for the mass contain no reference to the baptism in the Jordan and the wedding at Cana, these themes are remembered in some of the texts in the offices. The most striking example is the antiphon to the Magnificat, which gathers them up in remarkable brevity:

66

'We keep this day holy in honour of three miracles: this day a star led the wise men to the manger; this day water was turned into wine at the marriage feast; this day Christ chose to be baptized by John in the Jordan, for our salvation. Alleluia.'

References to the *tria miracula* are found in other places.[5] The office hymn by Sedulius, dating from the fifth century, mentions them in successive verses:

> *The eastern sages saw from far*
> *And followed on his guiding star;*
> *By light their way to Light they trod,*
> *And by their gifts confessed their God.*
>
> *Within the Jordan's sacred flood*
> *The heavenly Lamb in meekness stood;*
> *That he who knew no sin that day*
> *His people's sin might wash away.*
>
> *And O what miracle divine,*
> *When water reddened into wine!*
> *He spake the word, and forth it flowed*
> *In streams that nature ne'er bestowed.*
>
> *(A. & M. Revised, 74.)*

Bishop Christopher Wordsworth caught the meaning of the feast in his magnificent Epiphany hymn:

> *Manifested by the star*
> *To the sages from afar . . .*
> *Manifest at Jordan's stream,*
> *Prophet, Priest, and King supreme;*
> *And at Cana wedding-guest*
> *In thy Godhead manifest. . . .*
>
> *(A. & M. Revised, 81.)*

And an antiphon at Lauds recalls the marriage-in-Jordan theme expounded by the eastern Fathers: 'Today the Church is united with her heavenly Spouse, as in the waters of Jordan Christ cleanses her from her sins.'

---

[5] e.g., see R. Tatlock, *An English Benedictional (Studies in Christian Worship II,* 1964), p. 34. As early as Paulinus, Bishop of Nola (*d.* 431), there were references to the *tria miracula* in the West—though this see in Spain probably followed Gallican customs (see pp. 28ff. above).

We ought to add that the Latin rite also possesses a form of 'Blessing of the Waters on the Eve of the Epiphany' after the Orthodox pattern. When it was revised at the end of the nineteenth century, however, the point of the ceremony was sadly obscured as it was reduced to a mere office for the blessing of holy water.

*   *   *   *   *

In their zeal for simplicity, the English reformers swept away a good deal of the material we have been examining. The First Prayer Book of Edward VI (1549) retained two of the three formularies for Christmas in the missal, minus their chants, secret and postcommunion (but with introit psalms); in the Second Prayer Book (1552) these were reduced to one (without an introit psalm). The epistle and gospel, which remain down to our own time, are those of the mass of the day, Hebrews 1: 1–12 and John 1: 1–14. The collect was a new composition, perhaps inspired by an *oratio* for Christmas I in the Gregorian Sacramentary; as we have pointed out, it recapitulates the themes of the feast by praying that 'we being regenerate and made thy children by adoption and grace, may daily be renewed by thy Holy Spirit.' The title, *The Nativity of our Lord, or the Birthday of Christ, commonly called Christmas*, was added in 1661 by John Cosin, Bishop of Durham, who was one of those responsible for the revision of the Prayer Book. (It was he who objected to the title, *The Epiphany, or the Manifestation of Christ to the Gentiles*, on the grounds that the festival really celebrated the manifestation *of God* in Christ.)

The reformers settled for the doctrinal rather than the historical Christmas gospel, making the Prayer Book celebration very much a feast of the Nicene dogma. The narratives of the nativity were used as the readings at morning and evening prayer. As in the Roman offices, Isaiah provided all the Old Testament lessons for both morning and evening prayer at Christmas and Epiphany in all the lectionary revisions undertaken by the Church of England—1549, 1871, 1922 and 1961. The story of the shepherds has been read as the second lesson at mattins on Christmas morning since 1871. Titus 2, the epistle for the midnight mass of the Roman rite, appears as the second lesson at evensong.

The proposed 1928 Prayer Book set a collect, epistle and gospel for Christmas eve. The collect is a translation of the collect in the Roman Christmas vigil and the gospel is that of the midnight mass (Luke 2: 1–16). The epistle is new, Micah 2: 2–5 ('Thou Bethlehem Ephraphah . . .'). These formularies have been printed in the *Alternative Services* (1966) with Isaiah 9: 2–7 ('The people that walked in darkness . . .') as an Old Testament lesson for the eucharist on Christmas Day itself.

The collect and gospel for Epiphany in the Prayer Book are taken from the Roman missal, but the reformers selected as the epistle Ephesians 3: 1–12, Paul's exposition that 'the Gentiles should be fellow-heirs, and of the same body, and partakers of his promise in Christ, by the Gospel'—obviously to emphasize the festival as a celebration of the Church's Gentile mission. The Roman epistle was used as the first lesson at morning prayer.

It is interesting to note that from 1549 the accounts of Christ's baptism in the Jordan and of the wedding at Cana have always been set as the second lessons for morning and evening prayer at Epiphany—an illustration to the reformers' sensitiveness to certain liturgical traditions, especially where the reading of scripture was concerned. In this way we also commemorate the *tria miracula* in the Church of England on January 6th.

VI. *Other Feasts of the Christmas Cycle*

St. Stephen, St. John and the Innocents

One of the minor curiosities of the Prayer Book is that the collects, epistles and gospels for St. Stephen's Day (December 26th), St. John the Evangelist's Day (December 27th) and the Innocents' Day (December 28th) are printed, not with the other saints' days after Trinity XXV, but between the formularies for Christmas and Epiphany (together with the collect, epistle and gospel for the Circumcision of Christ). The English reformers found them in this position in the missal, and they evidently did not feel that it was necessary to alter the arrangement. So the Prayer Book has inherited an adjustment which took place in the service books between the sixth and the eighth centuries, when the Christmas formularies ceased to be copied into the *Sanctorale* and were placed, with their attendant collection of saints' days, in the *Temporale*. By this time Christmas was coming to be regarded as the beginning of the ecclesiastical year—probably because it was near January 1st.[1]

Stephen, John and the Innocents were among the first of the New Testament saints and martyrs to be commemorated in the early Roman calendar. At the time of the Philocalian almanac only local martyrs were commemorated, but the Leonine Sacramentary expressly mentions these three days— though St. Stephen's Day seems to have been kept at the beginning of August (perhaps because the name was confused with that of Pope Stephen whose *obit* was the 2nd or 3rd of the month).[2] Once they were observed, however, these

---

[1] In the Leonine Sacramentary (*c*. 560) Christmas is found at the end of the liturgical year among the December saints' days. It was only during the second half of the sixth century that Rome fixed Christmas Day as the beginning of the ecclesiastical calendar. The Gelasian Sacramentary puts the *Orationes et Preces in Vigiliis Natalis Domini* first in the year.

[2] W. H. Frere, *Studies in Early Roman Liturgy—the Kalendar* (1930), pp. 31–2.

three days—together with others that we shall examine in this chapter—were so associated with the Christmas cycle of feasts that their formularies were always kept together when new service books were produced.

The lessons for St. Stephen's Day underline the imitation of Christ which is the heart of the martyr's witness. The Roman epistle is the account in Acts of Stephen's ministry (6: 8–10) and death (7: 54–60); the Prayer Book epistle is the latter passage (beginning at verse 55) which includes the Christ-like prayer for the persecutors, 'Lord, lay not this sin to their charge.' The gospel in both the missal and the Prayer Book is Jesus' reproach to the scribes: 'Behold, I send unto you prophets, and wise men, and scribes, and some of them ye shall kill and crucify. . . . O Jerusalem, Jerusalem, thou that killest the prophets, and stonest them which are sent unto thee . . .' (Matthew 23: 34–9).

The chants are verses from Psalms 6 and 119 and from the account of the martyrdom: 'Princes did sit, and speak against me, and the wicked persecuted me: help me, O Lord my God, for thy servant is occupied in thy commandments' (introit antiphon and gradual); 'I see the heavens opened, and Jesus standing on the right hand of the power of God' (alleluia verse and communion); 'The apostles chose Stephen the Levite, a man full of faith and of the Holy Ghost: whom the Jews stoned as he prayed, saying, Lord Jesus, receive my spirit, alleluia' (offertory).

The Roman collect speaks of 'celebrating the heavenly birthday of him who could plead even for his persecutors,' but in the Prayer Book the present version, modified by Cosin in 1661, is addressed to Jesus Christ (perhaps deliberately copying Stephen's own prayer) that 'in all our sufferings here upon earth, for the testimony of thy truth, we may stedfastly look up to heaven,' following the martyr's example. The close connection between this feast day and that which precedes it strengthens the implication that the protomartyr trod in his Master's footsteps.

Although December 27th is the feast of St. John Apostle and Evangelist in the missal, its parent in the Leonine Sacramentary and the Sacramentary of Autun is a commemoration of James *and* John. This double observance is the result of a tradition that the apostle suffered martyrdom in Jerusalem at the same time as his brother, James. The Lectionary of

71

Luxeuil assigns to it as a gospel Mark 10: 35ff., where the two brothers are mentioned ('And James and John, the sons of Zebedee, came unto him, saying, Master, we would that thou shouldest do for us whatsoever we shall desire . . . '). But the missal commemorates John, not as a martyr, but as an evangelist—or, rather, as a theologian, for the epistle is the passage from Ecclesiasticus 15 from which is taken the chant for the common of doctors of the Church: 'In the midst of the Church the Lord opened his mouth: and he filled him with the spirit of wisdom and understanding: in a robe of glory he arrayed him.' The gospel is the Johannine guarantee: 'This is the disciple which testifieth of these things, and wrote these things, and we know that his testimony is true. . . .' The introit is from the epistle; the other chants are from the gospel pericope and Psalm 92.

The English reformers substituted another New Testament passage of Johannine witness for the epistle (1 John 1: 'And these things we write unto you, that your joy may be full') and translated the collect with great skill: 'Merciful Lord, we beseech thee to cast thy bright beams of light upon thy Church, that it may be enlightened by the doctrine of the blessed apostle and evangelist. . . .' It harmonizes with the general character of the Christmas cycle as the season of light.

Tragedies involving children are familiar enough in every age to give a sad poignancy to the commemoration on December 28th, but the sorrow of the Church finds expression only in the account of the massacre read as the gospel and in the communion chant, which repeats the prophecy quoted by Matthew: 'In Rama, a voice was heard, lamentation and mourning: Rachel weeping for her children, and would not be comforted, because they are not.' Elsewhere in the formularies, there rings out the note of thankfulness and triumph at the witness of the Holy Innocents, the youngest martyrs for Christ. 'Out of the mouths of babes, O God, and of sucklings, hast thou perfected praise because of thine enemies,' sings the introit antiphon; 'O Lord our Governor, how excellent is thy name in all the world,' cries the introit from the same Psalm 8; 'Praise the Lord, ye children,' continues the alleluia verse, on the days when it is used, 'O praise the name of the Lord.'

For those who lose their young there is always the hope of

their maturity and fulfilment in the care of their heavenly Father, safe from the evil of the world, so the gradual and offertory are from Psalm 124: 'Our soul is escaped, even as a bird out of the snare of the fowler: the snare is broken, and we are delivered.' The epistle is the vision of the throne of the Lamb with the saints from the Apocalypse: 'These were the redeemed from among men, being the firstfruits unto God, and to the Lamb: and in their mouth was found no guile: for they are without fault before the throne of God.' Fittingly, in the recent Roman revisions the liturgical colour was changed from purple to white.

Thomas Becket was canonized in 1173, three years after his murder, but his name was struck out of the calendar by Henry VIII in a campaign to obliterate the memory of this defiant churchman. St. Silvester (January 31st), the oldest of the commemorations in the days immediately after Christmas, was given a 'black letter' status.

The Circumcision of Christ

The celebration of our Lord's nativity turned the Church's devout attention to that other figure in the scene at Bethlehem, the Virgin Mary. Ambrose interpreted a verse in Psalm 19 allegorically as a reference to our Lady: 'As a cloud she waters the earth with the rain of Christ's grace. For it has been written of her, "Lo, the Lord cometh seated upon a light cloud." ' In their Christmas sermons Augustine and Leo frequently pointed to her as a model of dedicated virginity and as a type of the Church. 'The Church, too, like Mary has perpetual virginity and inviolate fecundity,' said Augustine, 'for what Mary has merited in the flesh, the Church has preserved in the soul (*in mente*).' Leo, in commenting on Isaiah 11: 1, thought he saw a mark of divine inspiration in the use of the word 'rod' ('A rod shall come forth from the root of Jesse'): 'In which rod (*virga*), no doubt, the Blessed Virgin (*Virgo*) Mary is predicted, who sprung from the stock of Jesse and David, and made fertile by the Holy Spirit, brought forth a new flower of human life, becoming a virgin mother.' [3] To us it looks uncommonly like a donnish pun!

As the Mother of God, Mary was the vital witness to the union of the divine and human natures in Jesus Christ, and

[3] NPNF, 12, 134.

references to her appeared in credal formularies and prayers at a very early date. 'Born of the Virgin Mary' is found in second century statements of faith, and before the time of Leo the phrase about 'venerating the memory of the glorious and ever Virgin Mary, Mother of our God and Lord, Jesus Christ' was included in the canon of the mass. The direct invocation of Mary probably began in Egypt during the Nestorian controversy over the *Theotokos* title. In the Church of Axum, a daughter Church of Alexandria, an Ethiopic hymn was sung which included the words:

> 'Blessed art thou of women, and blessed is the fruit of thy womb. . . .
> All the saints shall say to thee, as is their due,
> Pray for us, O thou who art full of grace.' [4]

In the west, the earliest form of devotion to Mary was expressed in church dedications. Sixtus III had inscribed on the walls of the rebuilt Liberian basilica: 'Virgin Mary, it is to thee that I, Sixtus, have dedicated this temple.' [5] This church was specially connected with the celebration of Christmas in Rome.

As New Year's Day, January 1st, was one of the popular holidays, the Fathers uttered severe warnings about it. Augustine's sermons for that day criticized those members of the congregation who joined in the junketing with pagans, and the early sacramentaries proscribed as counter measures penitential fasts, litanies and processions for that day, together with a mass *ad prohibendum ab idolis*.

In the late seventh or early eighth century, however, some Roman sources indicate that this day was also kept as the *Natale S. Mariae*—perhaps one of the most primitive of all Marian festivals. Traces of this commemoration still appear in the formularies in the missal: the station for the mass is St. Mary in Trastevere, the collect refers to 'the fruitful virginity of blessed Mary,' and the antiphons to the psalms and the Magnificat in the office all speak of Mary's part in God's redeeming work—she is the obedient servant of the *admirabile commercium,* the burning bush which contained

---

[4] P. Palmer, *Mary in the Documents of the Church* (1954), p. 54.
[5] The Hieronymian Martyrology (fifth century) gives the date of this dedication as August 5th—a day which is still a Marian festival in the Roman missal.

the presence of God, the rod of Jesse, and the temple of the Lord.

But at some stage in its history the focus of this festival shifted away from Mary to the circumcision of the child. This was undoubtedly caused by the reference in scripture to the fact that Jesus was circumcised 'when eight days were accomplished.' The custom of distinguishing festivals by giving them an octave began in the fourth century, and as January 1st is eight days after Christmas, the tendency to keep it as the *octava Domini* grew stronger. The Lucan narrative of the circumcision became the gospel for the day. In the latest Roman revision, however, it has once more become the *octava Nativitatis*—the title of 'Circumcision' has disappeared. The dependence of this octave day on Christmas is reflected in the repetition of the epistle of the midnight mass (Titus 2: 11–15) and in the use of the chants (the introit and its antiphon, the gradual, the offertory and the communion are all taken from the third Christmas mass; the alleluia verse is the opening sentence of the epistle from the same mass).

The Gelasian Sacramentary has a preface for the octave of Christmas which was obviously used at a time when January 1st mirrored the preceding festival. It refers to many of the events connected with the appearing of Christ and to the paradox of the Incarnation:

'As we celebrate today the octave of his birth, we revere the marvels you wrought, Lord, when he was born: for she that gave him birth was a virgin mother, and he that was born of her was a child of God. No wonder was it that the heavens gave tongue, the angels rejoiced, the magi underwent a transformation, kings were seized with anxiety, and tiny children were crowned with the glory of martyrdom. He was our Food, yet his mother fed him; he was the Bread that came from heaven, yet he was laid in a manger like fodder, for the animals to eat devoutly. There did the ox recognize its Owner and the ass its Master's crib: there did the people of the circumcision acknowledge him, there did the Gentiles acclaim him. This figure too did our Lord fulfil to the utmost, when of his kindness he was taken in Simeon's arms in the temple. Therefore with angels and archangels. . . .'[6]

[6] Preface for the Octave of Christmas, quoted in A. Hamman, *Early Christian Prayers* (Eng. tr. 1961), pp. 246–7. Text in H. B. Wilson (H.B.S., 1894), p. 9.

The English reformers kept the gospel for the day but composed a new collect about 'the true circumcision of the Spirit' [7] and substituted Romans 4: 8–14, Paul's discussion about Abraham's circumcision, as an epistle. The result, as F. E. Brightman commented, is that they turned the feast into 'a commemoration of circumcision rather than of the Circumcision of our Lord.' The 1928 Prayer Book added a collect for the beginning of the new year.

The Feast of the Holy Name and the Commemoration of the Baptism of our Lord Jesus Christ

The feast of the Holy Name of Jesus (January 2nd) appeared in some liturgical books from the fourteenth century onwards; but it was not sufficiently established in England at the time of the Reformation to find its way into the Prayer Book, and it was not observed universally in the Roman Catholic Church until the eighteenth century. The gospel repeats the last verse of the reading for the previous day, 'When eight days were accomplished for the circumcising of the child: his name was called Jesus, which was so named of the angel before he was conceived in the womb'; the epistle is Acts 4: 8–12, the part of Peter's speech before the high priest in which he claims that the impotent man had been healed 'by the name of Jesus Christ of Nazareth, whom ye crucified.' The chants, from the Psalms and Philippians 2, skilfully ring the changes round the names of 'Jesus' and 'Lord.'

In the 1955 revisions of the Roman rite, the octave day of the Epiphany was renamed *The Commemoration of the Baptism of our Lord Jesus Christ*. This particular day has always had St. John's account of the baptism in the Jordan as its gospel. The remainder of the formularies, except the collects, are those of the feast of Epiphany. It is a pity that the Congregation of Rites did not use the opportunity to choose a suitable epistle and chants related to the event.

The Presentation of Christ in the Temple

A number of feasts take their dates in the year from Christmas Day—the Annunciation on March 25th, the Nativity of John the Baptist on June 25th, etc.—but the last festival of

[7] It was probably adapted from a 'benediccio' in the *Missale adusum ecclesie Westmonasteriensis*, H.B.S., 5 (1893), c. 540. F. E. Brightman, *The English Rite* (1915), p. xcv.

the Christmas cycle is on February 2nd, the Presentation of Christ in the Temple.

Like the feast of the Circumcision, it has changed its character somewhat during the centuries. When it was first celebrated in Jerusalem during the fourth century, its theme was the presentation of Christ in the temple.

'Without doubt,' wrote the indefatigable Egeria, 'the fortieth day after the Epiphany is celebrated here with the very highest honour, for on that day there is a procession . . . and all things are done with the greatest joy, just as at Easter. All the priests preach, and then the bishop, always taking for their subject that part of the Gospel where Joseph and Mary brought the Lord into the temple on the fortieth day, and Simeon and Anna the prophetess, the daughter of Phanuel, saw him. . . .'

In eastern liturgies it has kept its old title, *Hypapante,* 'the meeting,' and this title was used in the Roman service books when the feast was observed in the west in the eighth century—though the date was adjusted to fit in with the western celebration of Christ's nativity.

The title demonstrates the purpose of the feast—to celebrate the meeting with the Jews as another manifestation of God, 'the theophany of the fortieth day,' as it was sometimes called. The incarnate Lord comes to Jerusalem to be accepted by the devout souls who wait for the consolation of Israel: Simeon blesses God for revealing to him 'a light to lighten the Gentiles and the glory of thy people Israel'; Anna gives thanks and speaks of him to all who look for redemption. In spite of the ultimate rejection of Christ by the ancient people of God, there were true servants among them who recognized the advent of the Saviour. The offering of the doves or pigeons for Mary's ritual purification in obedience to the Mosaic law was only the occasion for this manifestation, not an essential part of it.

The formularies in the Roman missal are chosen with the mystery of the *hypapante* in mind. The epistle is from the prophet Malachi, foretelling that 'the Lord, whom ye seek, shall suddenly come to his temple.' In the introit and its antiphon and in the gradual we seem to hear the thanksgiving prayer of Simeon and Anna in verses from Psalm 48: 'We have waited, O God, for thy loving-kindness in the midst of thy temple. . . . Like as we have heard, so have we seen, in the city of God, even upon his holy hill.' The alleluia verse ponders over the paradox of the occasion: 'The old man carried the child, but the child was the old man's King.' The proper preface is of the Nativity.

There used to be in Rome at the beginning of February an outdoor procession organized by the Church as a reparation for some pagan ceremony that defiled the city, and in time this became attached to the liturgy of the day. Candles were carried, giving the feast the title of 'Candlemass.' But the penitential object of the procession was remembered down until recent times: the colour of the vestments for the procession was purple until 1960.

Although the formularies for February 2nd are not those one would normally associate with a Marian feast, the growing veneration of the Mother of God in the early middle ages changed this day into one of the festivals of our Lady. The antiphons for the procession show traces of this transformation:

'O Sion, adorn thy bride-chamber, and receive Christ the King: greet Mary, who is the gate of heaven: for she beareth the King of the glory of the new light: she remaineth a virgin, yet beareth in her hands a Son begotten before the morning star: whom Simeon took into his arms, declaring to the nations that he is the Lord of life and death, and the Saviour of the world.'

The 1549 Prayer Book dropped the epistle and shortened the gospel, but Cosin restored these in 1661 and rewrote the title, *The Presentation of Christ in the Temple, commonly called the Purification of Saint Mary the Virgin*. His liturgical instinct was, as usual, very sound.

The Sundays after Epiphany

Although Christmas and Epiphany do not possess a following season—the Sundays are numbered after Epiphany purely as a matter of convenience in the west—echoes of the celebration continue in the formularies for some weeks after January 6th. The group of sacramentaries known as the eighth-century Gelasians provide a series of proper prefaces for the Sundays after Epiphany, giving thanks to God for redemption through his incarnate Son; but in the Roman missal and in the Prayer Book we can only detect these echoes in the gospels and (in the case of the missal) in some of the chants.

Epiphany I has the story of the twelve-year-old Jesus in the temple as its gospel (Luke 2: 41–52), a manifestation of God, himself the eternal Wisdom, to the doctors of Israel. The chants are from the 'epiphany' Psalms, 72 and 100, 'Blessed be the Lord, even the God of Israel, which only doeth wondrous things from the beginning' and 'O be joyful in the Lord all ye lands.' But the epistle has nothing to do with the feasts. It was taken from an ancient list in which there was a continuous reading from the letter to the Romans, a *lectio continua* which can be traced in the readings for the second third and fourth Sundays after Epiphany. In the eighteenth century this Sunday came to be kept as the feast of the Holy Family in the Roman Catholic Church.

The gospel for Epiphany II is the wedding at Cana, one of the *tria miracula*. The joy of the Christmas cycle is prolonged in the introit and offertory chants from Psalm 66, 'All the earth shall worship thee, O God, and sing of thee: they shall sing praises unto thy name.'

In the older lectionaries the gospel for Epiphany II used to be Luke 4: 14–22, Jesus' first sermon in the synagogue at Nazareth. Then the pericope was put back to Epiphany III to make way for the present gospel, and finally it disappeared from this part of the liturgical year. The only trace of it today is the communion chant for Epiphany III, 'All wondered at the gracious words which proceeded out of his mouth.' The third Sunday now has the account of the healing of the leper and of the centurion's servant as its gospel. The latter incident to some extent possesses the character of the western Epiphany in that it tells of a response in faith by a Gentile.

The gospel for Epiphany III (Matthew 8: 1–13), together with those for Epiphany IV (Matthew 8: 23–7), Epiphany V (Matthew 13: 24–30) and Epiphany VI (Matthew 13: 31–5), form another *lectio continua* from some ancient lectionary. In the Prayer Book these readings have been lengthened and Matthew 24: 23–31 added as the gospel for the sixth Sunday.

VII. *Advent*

Advent is an entirely western institution. Eastern liturgies contain certain features which might be interpreted as a preparation for the feasts of the Christmas cycle: the morning office of the Coptic rite has seven hymns in honour of the Virgin Mary, dating from about the sixth century, to be sung in the weeks before Christmas; the Byzantine rite reads the prophetic passages in the Old Testament which find their fulfilment in Christ's nativity; the Syrian rite includes two 'Annunciation' Sundays—the annunciation of Zechariah and the annunciation of Mary—in the fortnight before the feast. But there is nothing comparable to that season between Advent Sunday and the vigil of Christmas (December 24th) when the Church in the west looks forward to the coming of the Lord.

Two traditions lie behind Advent. The first arose in parts of Gaul and Spain; the second emerged in and around the city of Rome. Both these traditions affected the character of Advent as it is now portrayed in the formularies of the Roman missal and the Prayer Book.

The Gallican Advent began to appear at the end of the fourth century. In its original form it was regarded as a preparation for Epiphany rather than Christmas. A fragment attributed to Hilary, Bishop of Poitiers (*d. c.* 367) and dated after 360, refers to three weeks' preparation for the anniversary of the Saviour's *adventus*. As we have already noticed, the Synod of Saragossa (380) laid down in its fourth canon that no one was to absent himself from church between December 17th and January 6th. And there is a manuscript in a St. Gall codex in which a pious French woman urged a married friend to withdraw into a religious house for three weeks before the feast.

Christians may have been encouraged to prepare for the celebration of Epiphany from December 17th onwards because that was the day on which the pagan *saturnalia* began. But the appearance of the season may also have been connected with the practice of baptizing converts and children at the festival. As Lent took its place in the calendar as a time when the catechumens were entering the final stages of their preparation for baptism on Easter eve, so the Gallican Advent may have been the time when other candidates were being made ready for their initiation on January 6th. The Gothic missal has on the eve of the Epiphany a series of lessons similar to those used during the Easter vigil. Like Lent, then, the Gallican Advent remained in the Church's year as a period of ascetical discipline for the devout members of the congregation after the number of adult baptisms declined.

The influence of the pre-Easter season can be traced in the varying lengths of Advent in Gaul. As Lent was a forty-day fast, Epiphany also had to have a *quadragesima;* but since in the Gallican Church Saturdays as well as Sundays were non-fasting days, it was necessary to begin Advent on November 11th, St. Martin's Day, to complete the forty fasting days by January 5th. Hence it was known as the *quadragesima S. Martini,* 'St. Martin's Lent.' When Christmas Day became as important as Epiphany in Gaul, the period of preparation was adjusted to end on December 24th. Some time before 490 Perpetuus, Bishop of Tours, imposed on his people a tri-weekly fast from St. Martin's Day until Christmas eve, and the Synod of Macon (583) repeated his ruling. In his *Regula virginum* Caesarius, Bishop of Arles (*d.* 542) preached about a five-day weekly fast lasting from November 1st to December 24th, obviously an attempt to fit in forty days of fasting in the eight weeks before Christmas. In some parts of the Carolingian empire there was a pre-Christmas season of three months, beginning on September 24th, a day kept as the feast of the Conception of St. John Baptist (nine months before the feast of his nativity on June 24th).

Advent was not observed in Rome until the sixth century. There was no tradition of baptizing on the feasts of Christmas or Epiphany in that Church and so there was no necessity to keep a second Lent. Philastre of Brescia and Augustine of Hippo both mention a single day's fast before Christmas but nothing more.

The Roman Advent seems to have originated from an older observance, the December Ember days or 'the fast of the tenth month.' The Ember seasons (*Quatuor tempora*) go back

F

to the very early developments in the Roman calendar. During the Ember weeks the usual Wednesday and Friday fast was extended over into the Saturday and ended in a vigil and a mass in the early hours of Sunday morning. At first there were only three Ember weeks—in June, September and December. The March Ember days were added later. They served to recall the Church to abstinence at regular intervals throughout the year. 'We keep the fast of springtime during Lent,' said Leo, preaching one December, 'that of summer in Pentecost, that of autumn in the seventh month, and that of winter in this, the tenth month.' [1] It was customary to perform ordinations during the vigil and mass of Saturday-Sunday in Embertide.

The Roman Advent grew up out of this older observance, but as a liturgical rather than an ascetical affair. Only when the Gallican practices affected those of Rome did Advent begin to change. It acquired from the Gallican rite a certain penitential character—though not exclusively so—and there was a tendency for it to become longer. Gregory the Great fixed its length to four weeks, but the Gelasian Sacramentary provides six Sundays before Christmas and traces of the longer Advent can still be found in the lessons and chants in the Roman missal for the Sundays immediately before Advent Sunday.[2]

The character of Advent, therefore, is something of a mixture. It is a quasi-penitential preparation for Christmas, yet it is also a joyful time of looking forward to the Second Coming. As late as the twelfth century it was regarded as a festal season. The *Ordo Romanus XI,* compiled about 1140, lays down that the pope is to come to celebrate mass *honorifice* with his full entourage and wearing his crown. White vestments are to be worn and the *Gloria in excelsis Deo* is to be sung. It was not until the next century that violet coloured vestments were worn and the *Gloria* was dropped in imitation

---

[1] NPNF, 12, 127. The Roman year in Leo's time began in March, so the seventh month was September and the tenth December. See G. G. Willis, *Essays in Early Roman Liturgy* (1964), pp. 51ff.

[2] See the references to 'waiting for the coming of our Lord Jesus Christ' in the introit and epistle for the eighteenth Sunday after Pentecost and in the chants for the twenty-third Sunday after Pentecost. J. A. Jungmann, *Public Worship* (Eng. tr. 1957), p. 210.

of Lent.[3] However, the 'Alleluia,' replaced by a tract in Lent, is still sung in Advent, reminding us of the joyful origin of one tradition in the season.

This mixed character can be explained also by a different interpretation of Advent in the early service books. In the Gregorian Sacramentary, Advent was treated simply as a period before the celebration of the Lord's coming in flesh: it was called *Ante natale Domini*. In the Gelasian Sacramentary it was *De Adventu*. But in the Bobbio missal it has become *In Adventu Domini*.[4]

The reason for this was a shift in the Church's general conception of what constituted an *adventus*. In pagan times it meant the arrival of a god or of a great one at a particular moment in history. When the apostles healed the crippled man in Lystra, the city was swept by a wave of emotion into believing that 'the gods have come down to us in the likeness of men,' and the priest of the temple of Zeus brought oxen and garlands to offer sacrifice because he thought that the deities were visiting his city in the form of foreign wanderers. Some years later Nero arrived in Corinth from a ship and a coin was issued showing him in the form of Apollo coming in from the sea with the inscription *Adventus augusti*. The incarnation of the Son of God, celebrated at Christmas and/or Epiphany, was for the early Christian the one true *adventus* to be worshipped.

But in the Christian empire this pagan idea of *adventus* was forgotten, and it was replaced in the Church's mind as a reference to Christ's *Second* Coming. *Adventus,* therefore, came to mean the *parousia* rather than Christ's advent at Bethlehem. The Bobbio missal, which is dated from the end of the seventh century, seems to have been the first of the service books to have been affected by this change of interpretation.

* * * * *

The Roman missal was compiled in an age when the double character of Advent had become established. As the beginning of the ecclesiastical year in December brought the

[3] See Patrick Cowley, *Advent: its liturgical significance* (1960). The famous 'O' antiphons, sung at vespers since the ninth century, also remind the Christian that he is, in J. H. Newman's phrase, 'a man who waits for Christ.'
[4] LMD, 59 (1959), p. 18.

Church once more towards the commemoration of Christ's nativity, so the readings and chants pointed her members forward to the second coming and warned them to be watchful. Even the venerable formularies for the Ember Days before Advent IV are not just readings and chants of fasting and penitence; they have acquired something of the expectancy of the season, chiefly by using texts from the prophecies of Isaiah and gospels about the Virgin Mary.

The first reading and the epistle on Ember Wednesday, the epistle on Ember Friday, and four of the five lessons on Ember Saturday are all from those passages in the prophetic book which look forward to the advent of the Messiah: 'It shall come to pass in the last days that the mountain of the Lord's house shall be established. . . . Behold, a virgin shall conceive and bear a son. . . . There shall come forth a rod out of the stem of Jesse. . . . They shall cry unto the Lord because of the oppressors, and he shall send them a saviour. . . . Behold, your God will come with vengeance. . . . O Zion, that bringest good tidings, get thee up into the high mountain. . . . Drop down, ye heavens, from above, and let the skies pour down righteousness. . . .' And in the epistle on Saturday from 2 Thessalonians, Paul urges his readers not to be deceived by false rumours concerning the *parousia.* 'We beseech you, by the coming of our Lord Jesus Christ, and by our gathering together unto him: that ye be not soon shaken in mind, or be troubled, neither by spirit, nor by word, nor by letter as from us, as that the day of Christ is at hand.'

From Isaiah and the Psalms the chants echo the Advent expectation. Some of them summon God to come: 'Stir up thy strength, O Lord, and come, and save us'; 'Come and shew us the light of thy countenance, O Lord, that sitteth upon the cherubim: and we shall be whole' (introit antiphon, gradual and tract, Saturday). Others rouse the Church to greet the coming King: 'Rejoice greatly, O daughter of Jerusalem: behold, thy king cometh unto thee, he is just and having salvation' (offertory, Saturday); 'The Lord is nigh unto all them that call upon him: yea, all such as call upon him faithfully' (gradual, Wednesday). Within the season of Advent, the Ember Days have become additional expressions of the theme of the Sunday lessons and chants.

Both these themes are, as it happens, found in the gospel for Advent Sunday in the Roman missal, the Lucan apocalypse: 'And there shall be signs in the sun, and in the moon, and in the stars: and upon the earth distress of nations, with perplexity; the sea and the waves roaring; men's hearts failing them for fear, and for looking after those things which are coming on the earth: for the powers of heaven shall be shaken. And then shall they see the Son of man coming in a cloud with power and great glory.' But since this gospel was used on that particular Sunday as early as the fifth century, it does not seem likely that it was chosen because of its eschatological teaching. Rather, it was read because it goes on to stress the need for vigilance in the life of the Christian: 'And when these things begin to come to pass, then look up, and lift up your heads; for your redemption draweth nigh.' The epistle, which has accompanied this gospel from its first appearance, also emphasizes watchfulness: 'The night is far spent, the day is at hand: let us, therefore, cast off the works of darkness, and let us put on the armour of light.' When Advent came to be regarded as a time of the *parousia* as well as a preparation for the *natale Domini*, these passages aptly expressed its newer significance.

The chants for Advent Sunday are taken from Psalms 25 and 85. Both express the desire for holiness. Psalm 85 seems to originate from the days when Israel was expecting to return to the promised land after the exile. Psalm 25 is more personal in its tone. But together they enabled the congregation to declare their desire to obey God's commandments in expectation of his *adventus:* 'Shew me thy ways, O Lord: and teach me thy paths' (introit and gradual); 'Shew us thy mercy, O Lord: and grant us thy salvation' (alleluia verse).

Isaiah also provides texts for Advent II, but the gospel centres on the witness of the greatest of the prophets—John the Baptist. 'Art thou he that should come, or do we look for another?' is the question that he put through his disciples to Jesus—the question of every man as he contemplates the approach of Christ. And Jesus points to what the disciples see and hear—the fulfilment of Isaiah's prophecy of what was to happen in the messianic age: 'The blind receive their sight, and the lame walk, the lepers are cleansed, and the deaf hear, the dead are raised up, and the poor have the gospel preached to them.' (The pericope closes with Jesus' own comment that John was 'more than a prophet,' the 'messenger' of whom Malachi had spoken.) We meet Isaiah again in the epistle, in which Paul reminds the Church in Rome of the universal nature of Christ's redeeming work and quotes the prophet's saying about the 'root of Jesse' who would rise to reign over the Gentiles.

The station for the mass on this Sunday is the church of St. Cross in Jerusalem, a church just inside the old city walls of Rome at the point where they reach out eastwards south of the Via Tiburtina, and since the chants were assigned to this mass later than the lessons, it is probable they were chosen because of their references to the Holy City. Again Isaiah provides the introit antiphon: 'O people of Sion, behold the Lord is nigh at hand to redeem the nations: and in the gladness of your heart the Lord shall cause his glorious voice to be heard.' The gradual is taken from Psalm 50, 'Out of Sion hath God appeared: in perfect beauty,' and the communion from Baruch, 'Arise, O Jerusalem, and stand on high, and behold the joy that cometh unto thee from thy God.' It is as if all the prophetic witness from Isaiah to John the Baptist is focusing on the Holy City at her crucial moment in the salvation-history of mankind.

The fourth evangelist's account of the forerunner's message forms the gospel for Advent III, with its declaration of the immanence of Christ: 'I baptize with water: but there standeth one among you, whom ye know not.' In the epistle Paul reiterates the forerunner's message, but as one who has known the risen Lord and his victory and so who can call the Church, not to repentance, but to joy: 'Rejoice in the Lord always. . . . The Lord is at hand.' These verses of Philippians 4 are also sung as the antiphon to the introit. The Advent keyword, *Excita,* which opens three of the four Sunday collects, is heard again in the gradual and alleluia verse, 'Stir up thy strength, O Lord, and come and help us,' and as the congregation went to receive the sacrament they heard once more the assuring voice of Isaiah, 'Say to them that are of a fearful heart: be strong, fear not: behold, our God will come and save us.' The prophet is also quoted by John the Baptist in the gospel: 'Make straight the way of the Lord.'

Since Advent IV originally followed the Ember Days, no formularies were provided in the early service books for it, because the mass which concluded the vigil of the Ember Saturday night was regarded as the mass of the Sunday. The present texts came into the Roman rite considerably later than those for the other Sundays in Advent, and the compiler simply took over the gospel of the vigil mass, the Lucan account of the Baptist's preaching. With it he chose 1 Corinthians 4: 1–5 as an epistle. This is the passage which begins, 'Let a man so account of us, as of the ministers of Christ, and stewards of the mysteries of God.' When he selected it, the compiler may have had in mind those who had just been ordained during the mass at the end of the Ember vigil; but it is more likely he was influenced by the phrases in the last verses of the pericope, which harmonize with the newer Roman interpretation of Advent as a season looking forward to the *parousia:* 'Judge nothing before the time, until the Lord come, who will both bring to light the hidden things of darkness, and will make manifest the counsels of the hearts: and then shall every man have praise of God.' He borrowed various chants from the Ember Days, mostly from the Wednesday, and so brought into the Sunday formularies references to the third of the *dramatis personae* of Advent, the Mother of God: the Isaiah prophecy ('Behold, a virgin shall conceive, and bear a son: and his name shall be called Emmanuel') for the communion and the angelic salutation from Luke 1 as an offertory ('Hail, Mary, full of grace; the Lord is with thee: blessed art thou among women, and blessed is the fruit of thy womb').

The Christmas vigil with its mass formularies was first provided in a sixth century lectionary of Capua. Matthew 1: 18–21 is probably the original gospel for December 24th. The rather abrupt ending at verse 21 ('And she shall bring forth a son, and thou shalt call his name Jesus, for he shall save his people from their sins') may have been deliberate: lessons were sometimes cut short in this way to emphasize the last words. Joseph had been addressed by the angel as 'thou son of David,' and the saving work of Christ, summed up in the last phrase of the pericope, is seen as the fruition of the Davidic line, traced in the Matthean genealogy from Abraham. The gospel may have attracted the epistle which now appears in the missal. At one time, as we have said, Romans was probably read as a *lectio continua* in Rome from the beginning of December until it was interrupted by the emergence of the Christmas cycle and the Advent Sundays. But as the opening words of this letter refer to 'Jesus Christ our Lord, which was made of the seed of David according to the flesh,' it seemed to be the obvious reading as a partner for the vigil gospel.

The chants are full of encouragement: 'Today shall ye know that the Lord will come to deliver us: and in the morning shall ye behold his glory' (introit antiphon and gradual from the Exodus—a hint of the paschal interpretation of Christmas which we have already discussed); 'On the morrow the iniquity of the earth shall be blotted out: and the Saviour of the world shall reign over us' (alleluia verse—one of the non-scriptural chants in the missal); 'The glory of the Lord shall be revealed: and all flesh shall see the salvation of our God' (communion—Isaiah again).

In the sixteenth century, the lessons and chants for Advent were not uniform throughout western Christendom, and the English reformers copied out the formularies they were familiar with in the Sarum missal and other English rites. As a result, the Prayer Book collects, epistles and gospels are not quite the same as those in the present Roman missal. The Roman gospels of Advent I, II, and III appear in the Prayer Book as the gospels for Advent II, III, and IV respectively, and the gospel for Advent Sunday itself is the Matthean account of the entry into Jerusalem—an *adventus Domini* of a particularly significant kind. (The 'Palm Sunday' story was no stranger to the Christmas cycle, as we saw on p. 54.)

The season of Advent in the Prayer Book has been given an additional complication because the collects, which are new compositions or adaptations, have been based on themes taken from the lessons. The epistle from Romans 13 in the missal has been lengthened and a collect for Advent Sunday constructed round one of its phrases ('the armour of light')—looking forward to the celebration of Christ's birth and the *parousia*. This is in the tradition of the season. But the epistle for Advent II induced the reformers to write a collect about the holy scriptures ('written for our learning'). Furthermore, the Prayer Book epistle for Advent III is the pericope from 1 Corinthians ('Let a man so account of us, as of the ministers of Christ, and stewards of the mysteries of God') and the juxtaposition of this epistle with Christ's remarks in the gospel about John the Baptist, coupled with the fact that this Sunday comes immediately before Embertide, led the reformers to compose a collect about the ordained ministry. The result is that Advent II has become a 'Bible Sunday' while Advent III has changed into a day of prayer for the clergy. No doubt Sundays of this nature are very necessary, but is Advent the most suitable season for them? The collect for Advent IV ('O Lord, raise up, we pray thee, thy power, and come among us . . . ') is a free translation of the missal's *oratio* for the day.[5]

[5] The Christmas vigil was dropped in 1549 but restored in 1928 with different lessons (Micah 5:1–5 and Luke 2:1–14, taken from the Scottish Prayer Book).

VIII. *Reshaping the Christmas Cycle*

Nowadays Christmas is an uncomfortable time for the thoughtful churchman. As the feast approaches, he finds himself in the midst of an affluent orgy of spending and self-indulgence that is as far removed from the Christian purpose of the celebration as were the ancient *saturnalia*. Through the media of mass communication, he hears other churchmen voicing their doubts about the events commemorated, and as he watches his children stumbling through tedious Nativity plays at school, or as he joins in singing carols about angels from the realms of glory, he wonders just how much contemporary scepticism and the traditional paraphernalia of the English Christmas has smothered the evangelical impact of this holy day. Is it possible, he asks himself, for scientific man to discern without the eye of faith the wonder of the *admirabile commercium* which inspires Christian devotion and joy on December 25th?

Christmas became popular in that highly privileged age when all the civilized and semi-civilized world was seeking initiation into the Christian fellowship; and for centuries, no matter how sternly she had to discipline her children against excesses, the Church was able to ensure that the celebrations on the feast day were directed reverently towards the nativity of Christ and God's saving mercy. Now this opportunity has passed. The spirit of Christmas has been swamped by the secularism of society and the world rushes by the crib—even when it is placed in the shop window or in front of the town hall. The beery *Adeste fideles* in the public bar on Christmas Eve or in the football stand on Boxing Day has nothing religious about it. Should we acknowledge that *Sol* has, after all these centuries, reconquered his old festival and that what the Church once baptized for her own liturgy has now apostatized unforgivably to paganism? Should we pull down our posters about putting Christ back into Christmas and scale down our parochial observances with the excuse that every one goes away for the holiday?

The temptation to withdraw is strong; but to succumb to it would be to withdraw from the Church's mission of proclaiming the good tidings of the Word made flesh and of enabling man to be truly human in communion with God. If we are appalled at some of the ways in which Christmas is kept today, let us remember that this tension is only a small part of that continual war between good and evil in which the Christian is always engaged. We can no more sacralize Christmas Day—that is, put it into a separate religious compartment—than we can sacralize any other day of the year. We can only commit ourselves and all our days to God in the faith that through the power of the Holy Spirit the whole of time may be sanctified; and the tactics to be adopted for this mission are those of involvement, not of withdrawal.

There are many aspects of this that might be discussed. For example, we could argue—in the terms of the-world-is-the-agenda missiology—that a distinctively Christian ethos remains in the contemporary secular festivities at Christmas time: that the holy marriage of the Bridegroom and Bride is glorified in the strengthening of family ties which result when thousands go home for the holidays, and that God's loving-kindness is reflected in the many acts of charity associated with the season. Or—in the terms of pre-evangelism—we could speculate on the indirect impact of popular religious institutions like the service of nine lessons and carols from King's College Chapel, Cambridge, heard and seen by a hundred million listeners and viewers all over the world.

But here we must confine ourselves to the proclamation of the Gospel at Christmastide within the Church's eucharistic liturgy—bearing in mind that the ministry of the Word in the eucharist, like the ministry of the Sacrament, is the covenanted means of enlightening and strengthening the people of God for their mission in the world. Through the readings (and through the subsequent expositions and/or discussions about them) the Christian learns God's purposes for mankind so that in turn he may understand more clearly God's immediate purpose for himself. The worshipper's response to that Word, expressed sacramentally in the communion of the Body and Blood of Jesus Christ at the altar rails, is worked out in the business of daily living. The revision of the calendar and lectionary, therefore, can never be a mere academic exercise, for the reading of the scriptures is near the heart of the

91

liturgy, which in itself is the focus and inspiration of the Church's life and mission.

Modern revisions are designed to redistribute the rich theological content of the feasts of the Christmas cycle over the days when most people come to church. There may have been reasons in a former age for fixing those feasts on January 6th, January 13th, February 2nd, March 25th, and so on; but nowadays Sunday is the church-going occasion for most Christians, and so the revised lectionaries commemorate the ministry of the Forerunner, the annunciation of the Blessed Virgin Mary, the adoration of the magi, the presentation in the temple, the baptism in the Jordan, and the wedding at Cana on the Sundays before and after the principal festival. (Christmas Day itself has remained attached to December 25th up until now. But are there not good reasons—social and commercial as well as ecclesiastical—for observing the Nativity of Christ on a Sunday as well—say, the last Sunday of the year? The Church 'fixed' the commemoration of our Lord's resurrection in this way long ago.)

By adopting a revision like this, it would be possible to reach larger congregations with the narratives of those scriptural passages which unfold the manifestations and implications of the mystery of the Incarnation. Furthermore, those events which at the moment receive a somewhat detached emphasis at Christmas time—the Virgin Birth and the happenings in the cave at Bethlehem—would be set within the fuller context of the whole Gospel in the minds of worshippers. To look at it from a pastoral angle, it is difficult to impress on people that what the Church celebrates at Epiphany or on January 13th is just as important as what she celebrates at Christmas if the observance of these days is possible only for a devout few. For all its advantages, the institution of the evening eucharist is not likely to solve the problem of weekday commemorations in the increasingly complex conditions of modern social life and especially of employment. The Church would make it practicable for many more of her members to share in such commemorations if she followed the simple expedient of moving them to suitable Sundays.

The Church of South India revised its calendar along these lines in 1961, and now the Joint Liturgical Group, representing the Church of England and other Christian communities, has followed its lead in proposals set out in *The Calendar and Lectionary* edited by R. C. D. Jasper (1967). Since these proposals show very clearly the shape of things to come, they are worth examining as a conclusion to our survey.

The Group provides sets of three lessons—an Old Testament reading as well as an epistle and a gospel—for the eucharists on Sundays throughout the year in a two-yearly cycle. The preparation for Christmas begins nine weeks beforehand and the Christmas season is extended for six weeks afterwards—the new Christmas cycle.[1]

The ancient tradition of reading Genesis 1 on Septuagesima Sunday is boldly set aside (Septuagesima has, in fact, disappeared in their proposals) and the ninth, eighth, seventh, sixth and fifth Sundays before Christmas are concerned with the creation, the fall of man, the covenant of preservation (Noah), the election of God's people (Abraham) and the promise of redemption (Moses) respectively. In drawing up its lectionary, the Group decided that one reading in each set would be what it calls 'the controlling lection' and that this controlling lection would be chosen because it presented the theme of the day, the other lessons being selected to fit in with it.

During the Sundays before Christmas, the Old Testament lesson is the controlling lection. In the first year of the two-year cycle the opening verses of Genesis 1 are matched by the prologue of St. John ('In the beginning was the Word') and Paul's passage about Christ as 'the image of the invisible God, the first-born of all creation,' while in the second year the idyll of the garden of Eden is allied with Christ's conversation with Nicodemus on rebirth as a gospel and the vision of heaven in Revelation 4 as an epistle.

During the first five weeks of this preparatory period, special attention is paid to those events in Genesis which form the background to God's plan of salvation. This gives the congregation at the Sunday eucharist the opportunity of hearing of those great figures in the Old Testament whom the Church has long recognized as 'types' of the Saviour—Noah, Abraham and Moses. The New Testament readings are chosen to expound their significance in the light of Christ.

During the last four weeks, the prophetic voice of the Old Testament—principally that of Isaiah—controls the lessons.

[1] See Appendix A, p. 98.

The fourth Sunday before Christmas keeps its 'Advent' characteristics, for the prophetic passages about the Day of the Lord are—as we have seen—intimately interwoven with the theme of the *parousia* as well as that of the Incarnation. 'How beautiful upon the mountains are the feet of him who brings good tidings . . . who says to Zion, "Your God reigns" ' (first year) and 'My deliverance draws near speedily, my salvation has gone forth, and my arms will rule the peoples' (second year). The gospels are the prediction about the signs in Luke 21 (the gospel for Advent Sunday in the Roman missal) and the warning about the last judgment in Matthew 25.

The third Sunday before Christmas is still something of a 'Bible Sunday,' though its subject is the Word of God in the Old Testament: the accompanying gospels contain Christ's saying that the scriptures bear witness to him (first year) and his exposition of Isaiah in the synagogue at Nazareth (second year). The second Sunday tells of the preaching of John the Baptist: the Prayer Book epistle for Advent III ('stewards of the mysteries of God') fits in well with this subject and is balanced in the other year by the exhortation to Timothy to 'preach the word.' The first Sunday has as its theme God's promise to dwell among his people: the story of the annunciation is read as the gospel in the first year and the account of Joseph's dream in the second. Thus the reshaped calendar brings us to the threshold of the feast of the Nativity with a selection of biblical passages which focus on those historical moments between the creation of the world and its re-creation in Christ in which the steps in the divine purpose are clearly marked.

Christmas Day itself has two sets of lessons—the same collection for both years of the two-year cycle. The gospel now becomes the Group's controlling lection: the adoration of the shepherds in the first set of lessons (probably with the needs of the midnight mass in mind) and the prologue of St. John in the second. The *apparuit* passage from Titus and the pericope from 1 John on 'the love of God made manifest' (part of the epistle for Trinity 1 in the Prayer Book) form the epistles, and the Old Testament provides the familiar Christmas lessons from Micah and Isaiah ('O Bethlehem Ephrathah' and 'To us a son is given').

During the six Sundays following the festival, the gospels

are those passages which demonstrate God's manifestation in flesh in the opening episodes of Christ's ministry—passages which we have discussed in previous chapters.

Christmas 1 takes over the role of January 6th as a feast of light to the Gentiles. The adoration of the magi is the gospel for each year. The Old Testament lessons are from Isaiah —'Nations shall come to your light and kings to the brightness of your rising' (first year) and 'I will give you as a light to the nations, that my salvation may reach the end of the earth' (second year)—and the old epistle for Epiphany (Ephesians 3: 1–6) alternates with the old epistle for Christmas Day (Hebrews 1: 1–14).

One of the advantages of having a two-year cycle in the lectionary becomes apparent on Christmas 2. The gospels for that day alternate between the presentation in the temple (first year) and the boy Jesus in the temple with the teachers (second year). In this way, both the childhood 'epiphanies' are presented to the Sunday congregation instead of being divided between a weekday and a Sunday as they are in the Prayer Book (Candlemass and Epiphany 1). Christmas 2 in the revision becomes a strong candidate for a new 'Holy Family' day. The Old Testament lesson and epistle in the second year of the cycle make it possible to compare the obedience of Christ's earthly parents to the law of Moses (the Deuteronomic injunction about keeping the feast of passover is read, an injunction which entailed making a pilgrimage to Jerusalem) with the obedience of Jesus to his heavenly Father, through which we are able to cry 'Abba!' (Romans 8: 12–17).

Christmas 3 commemorates the baptism in the Jordan, the second traditional Epiphany theme. St. Matthew's account is read in the first year and St. John's in the second—another advantage of the two-yearly arrangement. The implications of the anointing of the Spirit in baptism is demonstrated in the story of Samuel anointing David and in Isaiah's logion 'I have put my Spirit upon him' from the Old Testament, and in the narrative of the Gentile Pentecost and in the Ephesian pericope 'God . . . made us alive together with Christ' from the New Testament. This collection of lessons enables the preacher to expound on that Sunday the universal implications of Christ's baptism, which have made this commemoration so important in the homiletic tradition of the Church.

Christmas 4 begins to move away from the Christmas-

Epiphany events with gospels about the call of the first disciples, but the third great Epiphany theme, the wedding at Cana, appears as the gospel for Christmas 5 in the first year of the cycle: its meaning is underlined by an Old Testament lesson from Exodus in which the Lord promises his presence to Moses and by an epistle from 1 John about 'the life was made manifest, and we saw it.' Finally the Christmas cycle ends with the themes of the sixth Sunday: the Friend of sinners ('I come not to call the righteous') and Life for the world ('I am the living water').[2]

The message of these Sundays might make a greater impact if they were given titles, following the Orthodox custom. Names like 'the Sunday of the Annunciation' and 'the Sunday of the Baptism' might well catch the attention of those who write and produce radio and television programmes with a religious slant. Dramatic, musical and documentary productions on these Sundays would proclaim their significance to a wider public in much the same way that the message of Christmas Day, Good Friday and Easter is taken up in different kinds of programmes.

Poets and composers would be encouraged to write new hymns for these occasions. (Perhaps one day the chants can be restored for ordinary parish churches in a revised and singable English Psalter in the style of the Grail-Gelineau version.) Artists would be commissioned to produce pictures, murals and stained glass windows on the themes. (Why not a series of 'Stations of the Epiphany' to replace the Stations of the Cross on church walls during the season?)

This admirable revision of the calendar and lectionary opens up many possibilities. But our immediate task is to assist the ordinary, thoughtful churchman to realize effec-

[2] Following the recent Roman revisions (see p. 76) the Circumcision of Christ has not been given any special prominence. It simply forms part of the gospel on Christmas 2 (first year). Perhaps I might add here that my only criticism of the excellent choice of lessons for the Joint Liturgical Group's reshaped Christmas cycle is the selection of the cleansing of the temple episode as an alternative to the marriage at Cana on Christmas 5. Although this is valuably linked with Solomon's consecration prayer and Paul's teaching in I Corinthians 3, I feel it belongs to the Easter cycle rather than Christmastide—in spite of its position in St. John's Gospel. A more obvious partner for the marriage at Cana is the miracle of the loaves and fishes (John 6 : 1–14), another of the Johannine 'signs' which speaks of the new order that Christ brings (see p. 58 above).

tively each year what it means when scripture says that in Christ all things are new, so that as he contemplates the theophany of God in flesh, recalled in the lessons at the eucharist at Christmastide, he himself participates more fully in the rebirth bestowed on him at his baptism. In this way, the reshaped Christmas cycle will not be just a more convenient way of reading the Bible to him on Sunday mornings. It will become the means by which he personally shares again in God's saving acts. For as the season comes round each year, he will be taken up into its *sacramentum salutis,* its mystery of salvation—that special grace which Leo the Great recognized in the liturgical feasts long, long ago.

G

Appendix A

A New Christmas Cycle

as proposed by the Joint Liturgical Group
in *The Calendar and Lectionary,* edited by
Ronald C. D. Jasper (Oxford University
Press 1967).

FIRST YEAR

9th before Christmas

Genesis 1: 1–3, 24–31a   'In the beginning'

Colossians 1: 15–20   'In him all things were created'

John 1: 1–14   'In the beginning was the Word'

8th before Christmas

Genesis 3: 1–15   The sin of Adam

Romans 7: 7–12   Sin and the law

John 3: 13–21   'God so loved the world'

7th before Christmas

Genesis 8: 13–22   'Be fruitful and multiply'

Romans 3: 21–6   'The righteousness of God has been manifested apart from law'

Luke 12: 1–7   'Beware of the leaven of the Pharisees'

6th before Christmas

Genesis 12: 1–9   The call of Abraham

Romans 4: 13–25   'The promise of Abraham'

John 8: 51–8   'Before Abraham was, I am'

5th before Christmas

Exodus 3: 1–15   The call of Moses

Hebrews 3: 1–6   Moses as servant, Jesus as Son

John 6: 27–35   Moses and the true bread

4th before Christmas
Isaiah 52: 1–10   'Your God reigns'
1 Thessalonians 5: 1–11 'The day of the Lord will come'

Luke 21: 25–33   'There will be signs'

3rd before Christmas
Isaiah 55: 1–11   The word from God's mouth
Romans 15: 4–13   'Whatever was written in former days'
John 5: 36–47   'You search the scriptures'

2nd before Christmas
Isaiah 40: 1–11   'Prepare the way of the Lord'
1 Corinthians 4: 1–5   Stewards of the mysteries of God
John 1: 19–27   The ministry of John

1st before Christmas
Isaiah 11: 1–9   A shoot of Jesse
1 Corinthians 1: 26–31 'God chose what is weak in the world'
Luke 1: 26–38   The annunciation

Christmas Day (i)
Micah 5: 2–4   'O Bethlehem Ephrathah'
Titus 2: 11–15   'The grace of God has appeared'
Luke 2: 1–20   The adoration of the shepherds

Christmas Day (ii)
Isaiah 9: 2–7   'To us a son is given'
1 John 4: 7–14   'The love of God was made manifest'
John 1: 1–14   'In the beginning was the Word'

Christmas 1
Isaiah 60: 1–6   'Nations shall come to your light'

G*

Hebrews 1: 1–4	'He has spoken to us by a Son'
Matthew 2: 1–12	The adoration of the magi

Christmas 2

1 Samuel 1: 20–8	Hannah's thanksgiving at the birth of Samuel
Romans 12: 1–8	Life in the body of Christ
Luke 2: 21–40	The presentation in the temple

Christmas 3

1 Samuel 16: 1–13	Samuel anoints David
Acts 10: 34–48	The Gentile Pentecost
Matthew 3: 13–17	The baptism in the Jordan

Christmas 4

Jeremiah 1: 4–10	'Before you were born I consecrated you'
Acts 26: 1, 9–18	Paul's witness before Agrippa
Mark 1: 14–20	'The kingdom of God is at hand'

Christmas 5

Exodus 33: 12–23	The Lord's presence with Moses
1 John 1: 1–4	'The life was made manifest, and we saw it'
John 2: 1–11	The marriage at Cana

Christmas 6

Hosea 14: 1–7	'I will heal their faithlessness'
Philemon 1–16	'I am sending him back to you'
Mark 2: 13–17	'I came not to call the righteous, but sinners'

SECOND YEAR

9th before Christmas

Genesis 2: 4b–9, 15–25	The Garden of Eden
Revelation 4: 1–11	Heaven
John 3: 1–8	Nicodemus and rebirth

100

8th before Christmas
Genesis 4: 1–10 — Cain and Abel
1 John 3: 9–18 — Love the brethren
Mark 7: 14–23 — 'What defiles a man'

7th before Christmas
Genesis 9: 9–17 — God's covenant with Noah
Romans 8: 18–25 — The glory to be revealed to us
Luke 12: 22–31 — 'Do not be anxious about your life'

6th before Christmas
Genesis 22: 1–18 — The sacrifice of Isaac
James 2: 14–24 — Faith and works
Luke 20: 9–16 — The parable of the vineyard

5th before Christmas
Exodus 6: 2–8 — 'I will deliver you'
Hebrews 11: 17–29 — 'By faith Moses . . .'
Mark 13: 5–13 — 'He who endures . . . will be saved'

4th before Christmas
Isaiah 51: 4–11 — 'My deliverance draws near speedily'
Romans 13: 8–14 — 'Put on the armour of light'
Matthew 25: 31–46 — The last judgment

3rd before Christmas
Isaiah 64: 1–5 — 'O that thou wouldest rend the heavens'
2 Timothy 3: 14–4: 5 — 'Preach the word'
Luke 4: 14–21 — The sermon in the synagogue at Nazareth

2nd before Christmas
Malachi 3: 1–5 — 'Behold, I send my messenger'
Philippians 4: 4–9 — 'Rejoice in the Lord always'
Matthew 11: 2–15 — 'Tell John what you hear and see'

1st before Christmas
Zechariah 2: 10–13 — 'I will dwell in the midst of you'

Revelation 21: 1–7	'Behold, I make all things new'
Matthew 1: 18–23	Joseph's dream

Christmas Day (i)
Micah 5: 2–4	'O Bethlehem Ephrathah'
Titus 2: 11–15	'The grace of God has appeared'
Luke 2: 1–20	The adoration of the shepherds

Christmas Day (ii)
Isaiah 9: 2–7	'To us a son is given'
1 John 4: 7–14	'The love of God was made manifest'
John 1: 1–14	'In the beginning was the Word'

Christmas 1
Isaiah 49: 7–13	'Lo, these shall come from afar'
Ephesians 3: 1–6	'The Gentiles are fellow heirs'
Matthew 2: 1–12	The adoration of the magi

Christmas 2
Deuteronomy 16: 1–6	'Keep the passover'
Romans 8: 12–17	'Abba! Father!'
Luke 2: 41–52	The boy Jesus in the temple

Christmas 3
Isaiah 42: 1–7	'I have put my Spirit upon him'
Ephesians 2: 1–10	'God . . . made us alive together with Christ'
John 1: 29–34	The baptism in the Jordan

Christmas 4
1 Samuel 3: 1–10	The call of Samuel
Galatians 1: 11–24	Paul's account of his call
John 1: 35–51	The calling of the disciples

Christmas 5
1 Kings 8: 22–30	Solomon's dedication prayer
1 Corinthians 3: 10–17	'You are God's temple'
John 2: 13–22	The cleansing of the temple

Christmas 6
1 Kings 10: 1–13	The visit of the Queen of Sheba
Ephesians 3: 8–19	'The unsearchable riches of Christ'
John 4: 7–14	The woman at the well.

Appendix B

The Christmas Crib

As early as the third century, according to Origen, the traditional grotto of the Nativity at Bethlehem was venerated by Christians, with a manger (*praesepe*) as the centre of devotion. Before that, the place had been a pagan sanctuary, for Jerome wrote:

'Bethlehem, which is now ours and which is the most venerable place in the whole world, was once overshadowed by the grove of Tamuz—that is to say, of Adonis—and in the cave where Christ once whimpered as a little child there sounded the lamentations of the beloved of Venus.' [1]

When Constantine's basilica was built, the roof of the cave was cut out so that visitors to the church could look down into the grotto. The cave itself was richly decorated and the manger adorned with gold and silver. It became one of the most famous shrines in all Christendom, and copies of it were made in other churches. This is how the Christmas crib originated.

The first copy was made in St. Mary Major in Rome. During the pontificate of Theodore (642–9) the supposed relics of the manger were brought from Bethlehem and enshrined in a special chapel modelled on the grotto. It is possible that the relics themselves were so arranged in the chapel that they formed part of the altar on which the pope celebrated the midnight mass. [2] In the early middle ages the church became known as S. Maria ad Praesepe.

Other churches followed suit. St. Mary in Trastevere had a manger in the ninth century. But little is known about the crib in early medieval churches. It is probable that they were connected with the liturgical dramas which were popular at the time and were introduced into churches in connection with these performances.

As an aid to worship, the liturgical drama was used origin-

[1] Quoted in Rahner, p. 149.
[2] They are now enclosed in a silver reliquary (sixteenth century) which is carried in a procession round the church on Christmas Eve and left on the high altar during Christmas Day.

ally at Easter, when there were processions to and from the 'sepulchres' on Good Friday and on Easter Sunday morning. These sepulchres, built to house the Host and a wooden representation of the cross, can still be seen in some of our older churches. The sentences printed in the Prayer Book before the collect, epistle and gospel for Easter Day were once part of a dramatic dialogue which took place in church between mattins and mass on Easter morning.

Similar dialogues came to be associated in medieval times with the feast of the Nativity. Old service books contain 'an office of the shepherds' (*officium pastorum*) which was used on Christmas morning with the clerks and the cantors taking the parts of angels and midwives.

A fourteenth century Rouen service book has an *officium pastorum* in which it is laid down that, during the singing of the *Te Deum*, seven youths are to vest in amices, albs and tunicles and to take their places in church carrying staves. A choirboy, 'stationed aloft' (presumably on the choir screen) and dressed as an angel, announces the Nativity to them (*Nolite timere*) and is supported by a chorus of angels who sing *Gloria in excelsis*. The shepherds walk in procession to the *praesepe*, which is set up behind the high altar, chanting *Transeamus usque Bethlem*. When they arrive, a curtain is pulled aside, revealing the figures of the Child in the manger and the Virgin, and they join in a dialogue with a group of clerks who represent midwives. Then they sing the introit together and the mass begins.[3]

Theatrical performances such as these were liable to abuse and they were forbidden from time to time by the popes. In 1207 Innocent III issued an edict against *ludi theatrales,* and this is probably why Francis of Assisi applied to him for permission to set up a crib in Greccio (and so unwittingly gave rise to the idea still widely held that he had invented the crib).[4]

Bonaventura described how in 1223 Francis obtained permission to erect a crib in Greccio to stir people's devotion. He tethered a live ox and ass in it with a supply of provender. Crowds gathered, and the holy night was made bright with

[3] The text of this office is printed in K. Young, *The Drama of the Medieval Church*, ii (1933), pp. 12ff.

[4] L. Gougaud, 'La Crèch de Noël avant Saint François d'Assise' in *Revue des Sciences Religieuses*, ii (1922), pp. 26ff.

lights and singing. The manger served as an altar for the midnight mass at which Francis sang the gospel and preached (it will be remembered that he was in deacon's orders). Other chroniclers tell of miracles connected with the incident, and a church was built over the spot.

The crib is now less important as a dramatic *mise en scène* than as a focus for private devotion. As always, its silent figures lead the Christian to ponder again on the mystery of the Incarnation, but the overall effect is frequently spoilt nowadays by the sentimentality, commercialism and downright bad taste connected with plaster figures, gaudy advertisements and innumerable Christmas cards.